Service-eLearning

Educating for Citizenship

Service-eLearning

Educating for Citizenship

Edited by
Amber Dailey-Hebert
Emily Donnelli-Sallee
Laurie N. DiPadova-Stocks
Park University

INFORMATION AGE PUBLISHING, INC.
Charlotte, NC • www.infoagepub.com

Library of Congress Cataloging-in-Publication Data

Service-eLearning : educating for citizenship / edited by Amber
Dailey-Hebert, Emily Donnelli-Sallee, Laurie N. DiPadova-Stocks.
  p. cm. – (Educating for citizenship)
 Includes bibliographical references.
 ISBN 978-1-59311-920-1 (pbk.) – ISBN 978-1-59311-921-8 (hardcover)
1. Service learning. 2. Telecommunication in education. 3. Distance
education. I. Dailey-Hebert, Amber. II. Donnelli-Sallee, Emily. III.
DiPadova-Stocks, Laurie Newman.
 LC220.5.S44 2008
 371.35'8–dc22

                                                                          2008013255

Printed in the United States of America

This volume is dedicated to student learners everywhere working to shape the future, and the service-learning practitioners who inspire and equip them for citizenship.

ACKNOWLEDGMENTS

The editors acknowledge all who contributed their expertise in service-learning and eLearning pedagogies to the development of this volume: Michael Beaudoin, Charlotte Boling, Kim Dooley, Carolyn Dunmore, Frank Farmer, Kristen Garrison, Louise Illes, Amy Kenworthy-U'Ren, Jean Mandernach, John Noren, and Marshall Welch.

Your review and timely feedback contributed vastly to the success of this volume.

CONTENTS

▪ PART I ▪

HISTORICAL PERSPECTIVES, CURRENT WORK, AND FRAMING QUESTIONS

▪ PART II ▪

SERVICE-eLEARNING APPLIED

▪ PART III ▪

MOVING FORWARD WITH SERVICE-eLEARNING

FOREWORD

Few topics provoke such strong opinions among academics as the proper role of technology in educational reform. Some hail technology-assisted learning as perhaps the greatest pedagogical advance since the invention of papyrus, predicting that it will more or less replace both the classroom and the campus. Others can hardly contain their mistrust of—or even their hostility to—an innovation that is forever "promising more than it can deliver" while consuming an enormous share of institutional resources. As is true in so many areas of contemporary life, the two sides often seem to be speaking past rather than to each other.

Among service-learning proponents, technology skeptics probably far outnumber technology champions. Several years ago when I was asked to give a "challenging" keynote at a service-learning conference, one that would force participants to reexamine their assumptions, I began by making a more or less familiar case for service-learning as key to educational reform. I then followed this argument with one that described the inevitable spread of technology-assisted learning, especially distance learning, and did so in such a way that the second argument indirectly but effectively undermined the first. The audience became so unsettled, it took considerable time for the group to regain its psychological equilibrium.

To be sure, few service-learning proponents question the limited, instrumental role technology can play in enhancing just about any teaching-learning strategy. Whether or not one personally chooses to use email, course websites, electronic journaling, online discussion forums, etc., such "tools" clearly represent a valuable resource for those who know how to use them. If a limited, instrumental use of technology were all the present vol-

Service-eLearning: Educating for Citizenship, pages xi–XXX
Copyright © 2008 by Information Age Publishing
All rights of reproduction in any form reserved.

ume was concerned with, few would find it controversial. It has, however, a more ambitious agenda. Its central concept—*Service-eLearning*—posits the need to approach the linking of service-learning and technology-assisted learning far less casually. Indeed, it proposes that such a combination establishes a distinctive pedagogy with its own epistemological and, hence, ethical implications.

All of us who have worked for years to move service-learning "from the margins to the mainstream" of academic discussion owe the editors of this volume a vote of thanks for putting the relationship between high tech and "high touch" before us in such a challenging way. Whether or not one agrees with the premises that inform *Service-eLearning*, one cannot disagree that the conversation this book seeks to advance is a conversation we *must* have if we are ever to effect serious educational reform. Unless those of us committed to such reform show ourselves open to inclusive dialogue, our efforts to make the academy more responsive to the needs of diverse democracies everywhere will in all likelihood fall short.

Edward Zlotkowski
Professor of English, Bentley College
Senior Faculty Fellow, Campus Compact

PREFACE TO THIS COLLECTION

The chapters in this collection evidence the rich potential of service-learning and eLearning to combine as pedagogies across the full spectrum of course modalities. Even when contributions speak from a disciplinary perspective, authors show the transferability of their experience across the curriculum and offer models for designing their own *service-eLearning* experiences. The collection is sequenced to provide grounding in the existing and emergent work to integrate eLearning and service-learning before moving on to applied models and general principles of practice.

HISTORICAL PERSPECTIVES, CURRENT WORK, AND FRAMING QUESTIONS

Our collection appropriately begins with two historically-oriented pieces. First, Amy Kenworthy-U'Ren reviews developments in the field of service-learning over the past ten years, as chronicled in the seminal *Michigan Journal of Community Service Learning*, the only peer-reviewed, national (United States-based) journal for service-learning scholars and practitioners. A research team comprised of representatives from each of three key stakeholder groups (student learners, community partners, and faculty) worked together to extract relevant issues and concerns from the extant literature and apply them to the domain of *service-eLearning*. Susan W. Post follows with a review of the existing research literature that links eLearn-

Service-eLearning: Educating for Citizenship, pages xiii–XXX

ing and service-learning. Post was invited to write this review of literature as perhaps the only doctoral candidate currently working on a dissertation in this area.

Randy Stoecker, Amy Hilgendorf, and Elizabeth Tryon's "Technology in Service-Learning: A Case Study of Appropriate Use" closes this section by asking: "When does information technology enhance service-learning and when does it inhibit it?" The authors provide a general set of considerations *service-eLearning* practitioners can use to determine the extent to which they want service-learning components to be technology mediated, technology assisted, or technology free.

SERVICE-eLEARNING APPLIED

Next we include several chapters which report on *service-eLearning* models across a broad range of course contexts and modalities. Jean Strait's work describes the "first generation" of *service-eLearning*, exemplified by Bemidji State University's Distributed Learning in Teacher Education Program, which combines face-to-face weekend meetings, fully online courses, and community-based service-learning placements. Strait argues that the "next generation" will include assessment to benchmark *service-eLearning* and traditional service-learning curriculum in terms of student learning outcomes. To that end, she offers Hamline University's *service-eLearning* program, with its rubric study comparing sections of the same service-learning course taught face-to-face and online. Strait concludes her chapter by reflecting on the qualities of effective *service-eLearning* experiences, qualities born out in the chapters that follow hers.

Kristine Hoover, Maureen Casile, and Ralph Hanke report on their study of a face-to-face service-learning course in which discussion board usage positively correlated to content mastery. A surprising outcome of their study, and one that should be noted in the design of *service-eLearning* curricula, this correlation was significant only for women. Their findings about the relationship between online communication and student learning gains are confirmed in the next two pieces.

Sandra Hill and Chris Harris assert *service-eLearning*'s value as a pedagogy for teaching professional writing skills. Their experiences suggest that *service-eLearning* not only helps develop students' awareness of the ways that writing engages democracy but also prepares students for the global eWorkplace. Christopher Blackwell, writing about how *service-eLearning* approaches can complement Community Based Nursing Education (CBNE), echoes Hill and Harris' findings about the value of *service-eLearning* to connect professional work and community activism.

Our final *service-eLearning* curricular model draws on myriad eLearning technologies. Hilary Kahn along with co-authors Sarah M. Stelzner, Mary E. Riner, Armando E. Soto-Rojas, Joan Henkle, M. Humberto A. Veras Godoy, José L. Antón de la Concha and E. Angeles Martínez-Mier incorporated eLearning technologies to facilitate communication, cultural adaptation, and learning outcomes for health professions students in an international service-learning course. Students and faculty from Mexico and the United States participated in web-based videoconferences to plan collaborative work, engage in team-building activities, conduct assessments, and teach joint classes. Analysis of student feedback on the experience confirms the potential of *service-eLearning* to transcend geographic and cultural boundaries to prepare students for global citizenship.

MOVING FORWARD WITH SERVICE-eLEARNING

Drawing on Thomas Friedman's (2006) analysis of the "flat world" and the cross-disciplinary competencies needed for meaningful participation within that world, Laurie N. DiPadova-Stocks and Amber Dailey-Hebert reflect on the ways that *service-eLearning* prepares students for increasingly "unscripted" futures. In these futures, the traditional formula of education = professional security = financial stability is no longer a given.

The emergent work in *service-eLearning* pedagogy presented in this volume provides a rich context for mining best practices. To that end, Emily Donnelli-Sallee and Amber Dailey-Hebert, in "Service-eLearning Best Practices: Possibilities for Engagement" sketch a set of best practices for practitioners who want to move forward with *service-eLearning* as an integrated pedagogy.

CHAPTER 1

SERVICE-eLEARNING AS INTEGRATED PEDAGOGY

An Introduction

Amber Dailey-Hebert, Emily Donnelli-Sallee, and Laurie N. DiPadova-Stocks

Service-eLearning is defined as an integrative pedagogy that engages learners through technology in civic inquiry, service, reflection, and action. The term *"service-eLearning"* recognizes educational technology as a powerful and value-laden approach to learning, and not simply as a value-neutral tool. As is clear, eLearning, in its varied forms, is becoming a fixture on college and university campuses, with the sheer number of online courses increasing at an exponential rate. Many faculty presume that service-learning is not compatible with teaching in online environments, resulting in the under-use of service-learning. As this book asserts, eLearning is not only compatible with but enhances and extends the aims of service-learning.

While readers of this collection may be familiar with existing work on service-learning and technology use, this book demonstrates the potential of a new model which acknowledges eLearning as a pedagogy within its own right. The new model presented here blends eLearning pedagogy with existing approaches to service-learning. The result is an integrated pedagogical approach: *Service-eLearning*. As the work presented herein highlights, *service-eLearning* responds to the challenges of today's rapidly-changing, technology-mediated reality.

The value of technology as a mechanism for enhancing the curriculum and administration of academic service-learning has been well documented in recent years (James-Deramo, 1999; Mills, 2001; Ogburn & Wallace, 1998; Saulnier, 2005). The blending of educational technologies and service-learning to date has primarily involved applying various technologies to course curriculum, positioning eLearning as *technology* applied to service-learning *pedagogy*. Representative of this important work is the Michele James-Deramo's (1999) collection *Best Practices in Cyber-Serve: Integrating Technology with Service-Learning Instruction*, which presents faculty testimonials about the ways that eLearning technologies such as discussion boards, online journals, virtual meeting software, and collaborative document editing can enhance service-learning experiences. This and other work connecting eLearning to service-learning points to the potential of eLearning to facilitate greater communication among participants in service-learning (Bennett & Green, 2001; Johnston, 1999); deepen the reflection component critical to service-learning (Bringle & Hatcher, 1999); and create alternative avenues for undertaking service to communities (Bjork & Schwartz , 2005; James-Deramo & Macedo, 1999; Malvey & Hamby, 2005).

The foundation of this volume is the theory and practice of service-learning. Building on that foundation, the book provides theoretical perspectives and illustrations to expand opportunities for global citizenship. Below we provide a grounding in eLearning pedagogy as essential knowledge for moving service-learning into the realms of online and hybrid learning environments. At the same time, this work offers eLearning practitioners an understanding of how service-learning can be an integral part of educating with and through technology.

BEYOND TOOLS: eLEARNING AS PEDAGOGY

Some service-learning practitioners explore ways to apply eLearning technologies to service-learning curriculum. Historically, educational technology has been viewed as a tool, mechanism, or enhancement. In its infancy, the practices surrounding Web-based or computer-based learning were just that—practices: "[m]uch online learning appears to have been developed because it was possible, technically, to do so and without explicit reference to any pedagogical principles" (Stephenson, 2001, p. x).

However, with this book, we attempt to shift current conversations about the application of educational technologies in service-learning from technology as *tool* to technology as *pedagogy*. eLearning has matured into a pedagogical approach to teaching and learning, rather than a mere modality (Anderson & Elloumi, 2004; Chickering & Ehrmann, 1996; Khan, 1997). This maturation is evidenced by book-length discussions that articulate effective pedagogical foundations for eLearning in higher education (Anderson & Elloumi, 2004; Stephenson, 2001) and betrays a larger epistemological perspective that sees the educational medium as inextricable from the process of knowledge construction engaged by the learner (Kozma, 1991, p. 197).

Our choice of term is "eLearning" rather than any number of other terms (namely "online learning," "hybrid/blended learning" or "distance learning") to underscore an important distinction. In using "eLearning," we recognize the broad spectrum of ways that technology and learning have been and will continue to be interconnected. The term "eLearning" has been distinguished in the literature from other terms as "the use of various technological tools that are either Web-based, Web-distributed or Webcapable for the purposes of education" (Nichols, 2003, p. 2). Our use of the term "eLearning" throughout this book indicates the use of this new pedagogy in a variety of modalities, including classroom-based (face-to-face), blended learning, and fully online courses.

SERVICE-eLEARNING: INTEGRATING PEDAGOGIES

In approaching *service-eLearning*, we build upon established definitions of service-learning as a "credit-bearing, educational, experience in which students participate in organized service activity that meets identified community needs and reflects on the service activity in such a way as to gain further understanding of course content, a broader appreciation of the discipline, and an enhanced sense of civic responsibility" (Bringle & Hatcher, 1995, p. 112). *Service-eLearning* meets these same ends, with the added recognition of the emergent role of technology in shaping how we participate in our democracy—as a means of gathering and acting on information about issues of personal and community relevance. This is demonstrated by the emergence of active, grass-roots participation such as discussion blogs on political issues and candidates, e-signature drives, Web-enhanced civic awareness and engagement (Drezner & Farrell, 2004; Foot & Schneider, 2006). Today's learners construct their views of public issues based on channels of information that did not exist ten years ago. Whether or not we as educators embrace these methods of gathering, reflecting on, and constructing knowledge, a new generation of learners already has.

Emerging from discussions of eLearning as pedagogy, and reflective of the essential dispositions fostered by service-learning, we derive the following *four pedagogical values of service-eLearning*. Nonlinear paths to learning, peer learning, global connectedness, and application. These pedagogical values synthesize eLearning and service-learning, weaving them into the new tapestry of *service-eLearning*.

- *Nonlinear Paths to Learning.* The traditional linear learning model, with the transmission and absorption of knowledge at its center, is increasingly a thing of the past. As nonlinear paths to learning suggest, self-direction and analysis of information are key components of the *service-eLearning* experience. New generations of learners have unlimited access to, and are expected to analyze, vast amounts of information within and outside the academy. As such, they must develop the dispositions needed to critically reflect and act upon this wealth of information, with a keen ability to cull the valid from the invalid sources of knowledge. Learners will merge and synthesize their experiences with their newly acquired understanding and perspectives, to construct an individual, integrated knowledge framework relevant to their personal context.

- *Peer Learning.* Another salient and unique feature of *service-eLearning* pedagogy is interaction with peers, experts and community partners using various modalities. Often in the form of online discussion, group work, and collaborative reflection, peer learning leads to knowledge construction as learners reflect, incorporate information from peers, and revise their understandings based on interaction. The structured exchange results in archived scholarly dialogue that develops a community of inquiry—a community characterized by open, authentic, respectful interactions. Learners will gain the diverse perspectives of others as they collaborate, exchange and resolve differences to pursue common goals of civic engagement. Finally, learners' perspectives are transformed as they assimilate the opinions and perspectives of peers and experts into a meaningful personal construct.

- *Global Connectedness.* When curiosity and passion compel us to further investigate a topic of personal interest, educational technologies provide the access, and freedom of autonomy, to do so. *Service-eLearning* creates innovative opportunities for civic engagement that extend beyond boundaries of time, geographic location, status, or context to serve the global community. As technology proliferates throughout our global society, *service-eLearning* is a natural conduit for connecting with others.

- *Application.* As learners synthesize the impact and results of their partnerships with others to better the human condition, they become well equipped, civically-responsible members of society at large. *Service-eLearning* cultivates intangible skills needed in a world in which our futures are inextricably linked, and empathy and commitment to human dignity become the impetus for transformative action. On a curricular level, *service-eLearning* incorporates authentic, relevant learning experiences. "Significant real-life problems, conflicting perspectives, or paradoxical data sets can set powerful learning challenges that drive students to not only acquire information but sharpen their cognitive skills of analysis, synthesis, application, and evaluation" (Chickering & Ehrmann, 1996, para. 26).

Table 1.1 summarizes the four pedagogical values of *service-eLearning* and the learner dispositions they engender.

We offer these pedagogical values and learner dispositions not to prescribe the nature or boundaries of a *service-eLearning* experience but rather to illustrate a framework for integrated pedagogy. It is our goal with this collection to advance conversations about technology in service-learning to the level of pedagogy, to encourage service-learning practitioners toward a view of technology as not simply a tool but as a *means* through which today's students learn. Adopting this view involves approaching technology incorporation within a broader context of eLearning pedagogy. *Service-eLearning* as a marriage of two pedagogies opens up possibilities for an entirely new learning model that utilizes the best of both fields to prepare students to fold technology into the ways they practice citizenship.

TABLE 1.1   Four Pedagogical Values of Service-eLearning

Pedagogical Value	Learner Dispositions
Non-Linear Paths to Learning	• Self-directed learning • Adaptability • Critical thinking and analysis • Problem-solving • Reflection
Peer Learning	• Collaborative exchange • Communication (both written and verbal) • Perspective transformation • Conflict resolution
Global Connectedness	• Personal investment in global social issues • Cross-cultural understanding • Ability to forge connections
Application	• Empathy • Civic responsibility • Synthesis • Commitment to human dignity • Creativity • Holistic thinking

▪ PART I ▪

HISTORICAL PERSPECTIVES, CURRENT WORK, AND FRAMING QUESTIONS

CHAPTER 2

CREATING PATHS FORWARD FOR SERVICE-eLEARNING

A Ten-Year Review of the *Michigan Journal of Community Service Learning*

Amy Kenworthy-U'Ren

The emergence of the term *service-eLearning* stems from the recent shift in our teaching environments—in today's educational systems, technology has permeated many facets of the teaching and learning process. Implementation and integration of service-learning into higher education practice have bourgeoned over the past twenty years (Kenworthy-U'Ren & Peterson, 2005; Lowery et al., 2006) in both international and domestic (United States) settings (Kenworthy-U'Ren, Petri, & Taylor, 2006). Considered "the dynamic education vehicle of our time" (Barnard, 2005, p. 24), eLearning is used in both private and public sector organizations for training and development (D'Cruz, 2003; Nisar, 2004; Welsh et al., 2003) as well as across all levels of education (Barnard, 2005; Friedman, 2006).

Service-eLearning: Educating for Citizenship, pages 9–22

9

To examine the interface between service-learning and eLearning, a ten-year review was conducted of articles published in seminal *The Michigan Journal of Community Service Learning* (MJCSL) between 1996 and 2005. The MJCSL is the *only* peer-reviewed, United States-based national journal for service-learning scholars and practitioners. It is a cross-disciplinary journal, with a focus on the critical examination, growth, and internationalization of service-learning application, innovation, and best practice. It was selected for this review as it provided a purely service-learning-based context for scholarship, focused on best practice and innovation, grounding the research review in historical and current issues in the field. A technology-oriented journal was not selected for the review, as the focus of that type of examination would be on issues related to technological application and innovation. The intention of this chapter is to maintain service-learning as the foundation, with eLearning as the proposed integration. Thus, the review is grounded in terms of historical service-learning scholarship, providing an opportunity for the members of the research team to derive their own insights and ideas about how the generic terms "technology" and "eLearning" would impact future service-learning processes.

This chapter reviews the past decade of literature on service-learning to extract issues that relate to the emergence of *service-eLearning*. Importantly, the review includes representative members' voices from the three stakeholder groups involved in all service-learning projects—university faculty/administrators, community partners, and students.[1] Each member of the team was asked to read through the abstracts of every article published in the MJCSL over the period 1996–2005 and to highlight those relevant to an educational and organizational shift toward *service-eLearning*. It should be noted at the outset of that, of the 155 articles published in the MJCSL over the period 1996–2005, only *two* (or 1.3%) of the articles referenced technology as a component of the service-learning experience, reinforcing *service-eLearning* as an emergent pedagogy worthy of inquiry.

KEY IMPLICATIONS FOR INSTITUTIONALIZING SERVICE-eLEARNING

Six key insights emerged from our discussion of individual member's issues as derived from the review process. The issues, presented in chronological order of discussion, are:

1. *Reflection will have to be adapted to an online environment.* For example, issues related to diversity and multiculturalism are common reflective components of service-learning projects; which may be much harder to process and understand over the Internet. How will stu-

dents explore these issues in a non face-to-face (f2f) environment? Designing effective reflection over the web may be a challenge as many service-learning practitioners often rely on small group f2f discourse. It may be harder to elicit intimate feedback from people over the Web. All of the nonverbal cues are missing from electronic communication, and they may be very important for effective reflection, particularly reflection aimed at self-discovery about sensitive issues (such as diversity, values, citizenship, perceptual biases).

2. *Shifts toward service-eLearning will invariably require a rethinking of projects' structural, operational, and logistical issues.* For example, will service-learning still be effective if it evolves from a slower f2f environment to that of a faster, Internet experience? Students and clients may lose part of the in vivo (in-life) experience if their foci shift away from f2f experiences toward Internet-based experiences.

3. *The population of involved faculty, students, and community partners will shift with the transition to service-eLearning.* The new eLearning mode may encourage new faculty members to become involved, but it may also force those who are already involved to leave if they are uncomfortable with the change. This issue may also reflect potential changes in nonprofit organization representative membership. Alternatively, the eLearning medium may increase the overall population of interested students, as it utilizes a framework they tend to be familiar with (Internet-based communication).

4. *Revised partnership resources and requirements will have to be monitored for effective community partner involvement.* There will undoubtedly be resource restrictions for agencies. Will nonprofit organizations be excluded from projects based on resource constraints? Technology requires more investment in some ways, and less in others. There will be community partner constraints about actual technological components, level of comfort, interest, and availability in online settings.

5. *Rethinking the benefits for nonprofit organization partners will strengthen partnership opportunities.* A potential benefit of *service-eLearning* is that social service agencies may become more accessible over the Internet (e.g., students can find agencies more readily, accessing information available 24 hours a day, transport options available online) related to the logistics of service placements. There is also a wealth of opportunity for students to work with community agencies to design programs and initiatives, source technological hardware and software, run training programs, provide information to clients and sponsors, facilitate outreach, and create online resources for community partners.

6. *Electronic journaling has the potential to add value for students.* Another benefit, strongly advocated by the student member of this team,

highlights that electronic journaling may well be easier for students. Students can access their computers and journals 24 hours a day, often through palm-based accessories. Most students today are also intimately familiar with the use of discussion boards and email; they efficiently and effectively communicate with other students using these media on a daily basis.

IDENTIFYING ISSUES OF RELEVANCE TO EACH STAKEHOLDER

Understanding the perspectives and needs of each stakeholder group is essential to designing *service-eLearning* experiences that benefit all involved. Below we present each team member's assessment of the most important issues related to the integration of eLearning into the service-learning domain,[2] as presented in the context of their article selections.

Community Partner

Article #1: Michelle R. Dunlap's (1998), "Voices of Students in Multicultural Service-Learning Settings," MJCSL, Volume 5, Fall: 58–67.

Article Summary
   The author presented themes derived from students' journal reflections following service-learning experiences in multicultural settings. In describing the project, the author focused on the importance of facilitating critical reflection processes through journal writing and in-class small group discussions.

Rationale for Selection
   The participating community partner was concerned that with issues as delicate and significant as diversity and multiculturalism (for example, ablism, gender, race, socioeconomic status), the potential absence of f2f reflection sessions (if reflection only occurs through online discussion forums) would hinder the quality of student interaction, reflection, and learning. There were also issues raised related to the percentage of the course that took place in an online environment, such that a fully Internet-based course would provide little control for the faculty member to both assess the quality and quantity of the service placement and would severely restrict the faculty member's ability to interact with the community partner.

Article #2: Sherril B. Gelmon, Barbara A. Holland, Sarena D. Seifer, Anu Shinnamon, and Kara Connors' (1998), "Community–University Partnerships for Mutual Learning," MJCSL, Volume 5, Fall: 97–107.

Article Summary

This article presented findings from a three-year national initiative called the Health Professions Schools in Service to the Nation Program (HPSISN), involving 17 colleges and universities across the United States. Using case study materials with a focus on qualitative data collection, trends and themes were derived from data collected across the 17 programs describing issues relevant to community–university partnerships.

Rationale for Selection

The community partner felt that the design of this research initiative, involving multiple sites with a longitudinal focus, was a useful benchmark for future assessments of university–community partnerships using *service-eLearning*. The member also thought that many of the themes identified in this article were applicable to the context of technological adaptation of service-learning projects. Of the six themes presented, the member highlighted four as relevant to *service-eLearning*; these include: (1) reciprocity and mutuality issues, (2) social and economic benefits arising from university–community partnerships, (3) benefits for the community partner, and (4) motivation for universities to respond to community partners' perspectives.

Article #3: Andrea Vernon and Kelly Ward's (1999), "Campus and Community Partnerships: Assessing Impacts & Strengthening Connections," MJCSL, Volume 6, Fall: 30–37.

Article Summary

In this research article, the authors examined community partners' viewpoints about the quality of student service-learning placements. After analyzing respondents' data, recommendations were made for improving service-learning partnership programs.

Rationale for Selection

The community partner identified three themes from this study particularly salient for *service-eLearning* program design. The findings from this study indicated that the participating agency directors and personnel felt that: (1) campuses are perceived positively in the community, (2) working with service-learning students has both challenges and benefits, and (3) more coordination and communication are needed from the university partners to create effective university–community partnerships. The community partner involved in this review cautioned that poorly structured integration of eLearning (i.e., integration that is rushed, ill-conceived, one-sided, and/or inadequately designed) into service-learning programs could do irreparable damage to university–community partnerships. Including eLearning into service-learning too quickly has the potential to exacerbate, rather than reduce, differences between university and community partners. Rather, universities should strengthen the positive perception community partners have of them through the thoughtful, fully-informed, communication-rich, and partner-based design of *service-eLearning* projects.

Article #4: Jeffrey P.F. Howard, Sherril B. Gelmon, and Dwight E. Giles, Jr.'s (2000), "From Yesterday to Tomorrow: Strategic Directions for Service-Learning Research," MJCSL, special issue, Fall: 5–10.

Article Summary

This article presented an argument for an increase in strategic service-learning research efforts.

Rationale for Selection

From the community partner's perspective, one of the keys to moving forward with *service-eLearning* is the immediate design and implementation of well-crafted research. Questions related to the impact of how eLearning will change the dynamics of students' relationships with each other and the agencies and clients they work with are paramount to successful program design. Additional research needs to be conducted on the quality of the students' learning and reflection, as well as the quality of the organizational outcomes for the partner agency.

Article #5: Nadinne I. Cruz and Dwight E. Giles, Jr.'s (2000), "Where's the Community in Service-Learning Research?" MJCSL, special issue, Fall: 28–34.

Article Summary

In this article, the authors called for increased *community-focused* research in the service-learning domain. They presented a four dimensional model for conducting research with community partners to identify process- and outcome-based issues. The four dimensional model included: (1) the university–community partnership as the unit of analysis, (2) consistency with good service-learning practice, (3) use of action research, and (4) focus on assets.

Rationale for Selection

The participating community partner offered that to be an equal partner in the design and practice of service-learning projects necessitated a clear and consistent research focus on the often overlooked community side of the service-learning partnership. This would become more important than ever with the integration of technology, particularly given the paucity of technological resources (including hardware, software, and intellectual/operational knowledge) available to some community partners. A great disparity may well exist between the technological assets of partners involved in future *service-eLearning* projects.

Student

Article #1: Floyd Ogburn and Barbara Wallace's (1998), "Freshman Composition, the Internet, and Service-Learning," MJCSL, Volume 5, Fall: 68–74.

Article Summary
The authors described a freshman composition course where students' service-learning projects involved the creation and online publication of local social service agency profiles. It should be noted that this was one of the two articles published in the MJCSL during the period 1996–2005 with a focus on technology.

Rationale for Selection
The student thought that this was an ideal example of technology applied to service-learning experiences. In this case, students' knowledge of the online environment was leveraged to provide a needed service to local agencies. The student team member for this chapter felt that most university students are on the cutting edge of all technological developments, suggesting their knowledge could readily be leveraged to provide much needed as well as technologically current services to local community partners.

Article #2: Ann E. Green's (2001), "But You Aren't White: Racial Perceptions and Service-Learning," MJCSL, Volume 8, Number 1, Fall: 18–26.

Article Summary
The author argued that in many service-learning settings, where a majority of the involved students are white and the agency partners and clients are frequently of color, a discussion of white privilege should be included as part of any course-based service reflection process.

Rationale for Selection
The student member of this team thought that this article reflected one of the most important, yet least addressed, issues related to university-based

service-learning programs. In this student's class experience, most of the service-learning students were white and most of them had not considered the practical, social, personal, and ethical implications of racial differences in service-learning settings. Her fear was that the integration of eLearning into service-learning programs would further reduce the probability that students would effectively engage in this type of reflection and processing. Article #3: Steven D. Mills' (2001), "Electronic Journaling: Using the Web-Based, Group Journal for Service-Learning Reflection," MJCSL, Volume 8, Number 1, Fall: 27–35.

Article Summary

The author described the use of a web-based interactive group journaling exercise as applied to student service-learning experiences. It should be noted that this was the second of the two articles published in the MJCSL during the period 1996–2005 with a focus on technology.

Rationale for Selection

The student team member thought that the application of technology to service-learning, as described in this article, was a laudable example of a carefully designed and thoughtfully integrated use of eLearning as a tool for reflection. She was impressed that the author ran the exercise for four semesters before submitting it for publication—an indication that the author had taken sufficient time to modify and improve the exercise as a service-based reflective tool.

Article #4: Julie A. Hatcher, Robert G. Bringle, and Richard Muthiah's (2004), "Designing Effective Reflection: What Matters to Service-Learning?," MJCSL, Volume 11, Number 1, Fall: 38–46.

Article Summary

The authors of this article examined the responses of 471 students asked to describe the quality of their service-learning course design, the nature of the reflection activities in the course, and the overall quality of their resultant learning. The results indicated that students perceived the level of integration of the service experience with academic course content to be significantly related to course quality. Students also indicated that reflection related to personal values, regular reflection experiences, and clearly structured reflection were significantly related to course quality.

Rationale for Selection

The student member of this chapter's review team felt that the inclusion of eLearning into service-learning experiences had the potential to dramatically decrease the perceived quality of the students' reflection experiences as well as the overall course quality. Given the multifaceted components of effective reflection, as identified by student respondents in this research study, the student felt that significant reviews of the extant literature on eLearning should be conducted before any integration was put into practice combining eLearning and service-learning. The student also had concerns about the quality of personal value-based reflection that would be possible in an eLearning environment.

Faculty Member/Administrator

Article #1: Richard Kiely's (2004), "A Chameleon with a Complex: Searching for Transformation in International Service-Learning," MJCSL, Volume 10, Number 2, Spring: 5–20.

Article Summary

In a study examining perspective transformations of students engaged in international service-learning, the author reported that students with international service experiences had "profound" changes in their outlook in at least one of the six dimensions: political, moral, intellectual, personal, spiritual, and cultural.

Rationale for Selection

Extending Thomas Friedman's (2006) conceptualization of the world as flat (that is, accessible at a historically unprecedented level), *service-eLearning* provides a new platform for engaging students in international service-learning experiences. The Internet provides a seemingly limitless world of information with continuous 24-hour access to people and places around the world. To date, however, research on international service-learning has been restricted to f2f service encounters where students typically engage in a short trip to another country to work with local people and service organizations (see Kiely, 2004; Porter & Monard, 2001). Anecdotal as well as empirical evidence of this type of student experience has strongly supported the continued use of these programs. *Service-eLearning* raises the question of how we can leverage the opportunities provided in an online environment to design Internet-based international experiences with similar student learning and agency benefits to those of f2f international service encounters.

Article #2: Valerie C. McKay and Patricia D. Rozee's (2004), "Characteristics of Faculty Who Adopt Community Service Learning Pedagogy," MJCSL, Volume 10, Number 2, Spring: 21–33.

Article Summary

In this research study, the authors identified a common set of characteristics for faculty members who are engaged in service-learning—a set of attitudes, values, and beliefs about teaching, learning processes, and the meaning of community.

Rationale for Selection

One of the issues raised with a transition to *service-eLearning* is that of faculty interest, engagement, and attrition. How will the use of electronic media for communication (e.g., Internet-based discussion forums, webcam, blogs, podcasts) impact faculty member interest in, and comfort with, designing and leading service-learning projects? Will an entire generation of service-learning practitioners be asked to step aside for new faculty who are more technologically proficient? Or is there a way to leverage the experience and passion of those who prefer f2f service-learning experiences, with benefits for those who are interested in exploring *service-eLearning*'s potential? The question of interested parties' characteristics extends to students and community partners as well as faculty. For example, Rick Sperling, Vivian Ota Wang, Janice M. Kelly, and Beth Hritsuk (2003) found that student characteristics influenced the social cognitive development resulting from service-learning experiences. A question arises, how will participant characteristics be different for students who excel in *service-eLearning* formats versus those who thrive in traditional face-to-face service programs, if they are different at all? What are the differences, if any, in the characteristics of community partners who are positively inclined to engage in *service-eLearning* projects versus those who are not?

Article #3: Lori J. Vogelgesang's (2004), "Diversity Work and Service-Learning: Understanding Campus Dynamics," MJCSL, Volume 10, Number 2, Spring: 34–43.

Article Summary

The author recommended a review of a university's institutional mission, campus leadership, curriculum integration, and organizational structure as a precursor to effective integration of diversity and service-learning.

Rationale for Selection

Institutional-level systems adaptation is a critical component of service-learning program success (Holland, 1997). To further an institution's commitment to quality service-learning program development in today's electronic environment, how much will we have to adapt our systems and processes to embrace *service-eLearning*? Is it possible for *service-eLearning* to prosper without campus-wide attention and commitment? And, if not, what type(s) of commitment will provide the greatest levels of assistance and support to ensure targeted, partner- focused learning opportunities for students and community partners? One example of the type of institutional questions raised by a shift to *service-eLearning* relates to selection and training—a critical quality issue for service-learning program development. With respect to selection, Mark Chesler, Jennifer Kellman-Fritz, Amy Knife-Gould (2003) identified four prerequisite characteristics of successful peer facilitators for traditional service-learning programs. One of the characteristics was "understanding of and skills in small group dynamics" (p. 59). How will the Internet as a medium for group dynamics alter the skills needed for peer facilitators? For faculty members? For students?

Article #4: Sarah L. Ash, Patti H. Clayton, and Maxine P. Atkinson's (2005), "Integrating Reflection and Assessment to Capture and Improve Student Learning," MJCSL, Volume 11, Number 2, Spring: 49–60.

Article Summary

The authors presented a model for tying assessment in service-learning courses, both formative and summative, to the reflection process. They argued that reflection "products" are an ideal vehicle for assessment when grounded in carefully structured student learning objectives.

Rationale for Selection

Reflection has always been a central tenet of effective service-learning programs, providing what many believe to be the actual connection or transition mechanism between students' service experiences and the outcome of learning (Eyler & Giles, 1999; Godfrey, Illes, & Berry, 2005; Hatcher et al., 2004; Jacoby, 1996). With *service-eLearning*, the major difference in terms of reflection from that of a traditional classroom setting would be the notable absence of f2f reflective opportunities. If structured well, discussion forums or online group portals may provide a similar level of opportunity for written discourse, although there may be timing issues (for example, students and faculty needing to be online together in synchronous forums rather than asynchronous forums) as well as the notable absence of nonverbal cues.

Article #5: Brenda K. Bushouse's (2005), "Community Nonprofit Organizations and Service-Learning: Resource Constraints to Building Partnerships with Universities," MJCSL, Volume 12, Number 1, Fall: 32–40.

Article Summary

In this article, the author examined which type(s) of partnerships were of most interest to nonprofit organizations. The author found that, because of resource constraints (for example, staff time), 64% of the organizations she sampled were only interested in transactional or "one-time only" projects, with the remaining 36% open to longer term, more sustained engagements.

Rationale for Selection

Brenda K. Bushouse's (2005) article highlights a fundamentally flawed assumption made by many service-learning faculty and university administrators—the assumption that community partners are desperate to engage in service-learning projects with universities. This hubristic "server and the served" mentality are contrary to everything that service-learning stands for, yet it has permeated much of the service-learning movement for the past two decades. It is only during the past 3–5 years that service-learning authors' and practitioners' attention has shifted away from a myopic "student-only" centered framework toward one that includes community partners' perspectives. One of the most cited frameworks for considering community partner perspectives involves a continuum starting with "transactional" one time events and projects on one end and moving to "transformational" programs resulting in joint knowledge and work creation at the other end (Enos & Morton, 2003). A second format for conceptualizing a service-learning partnership program is that of Silvia Dorado and Dwight Giles (2004). They discuss three "paths of engagement" for university and community service partnerships: tentative, aligned, and committed. Tentative engagements are those where "learning behaviors are dominant" and "partners are not interested in building a sustainable relationship" (p. 30). Engagements are aligned when partners "seek to create a better fit between their goals" (p. 31); it is a path that most partners will not remain on long, as they either transition to a committed partnership or dissolve their work together. Finally, the committed path of engagement represents those partnerships involving "actions and interactions that denote that partners value the partnership beyond the departing project" (p. 31). As emphasized by the community team member's article selections above (most relate to community voice issues), partnerships involve effective communication, trust, and respect. For service-learning to move forward into an eLearning domain, faculty and administrators must remain vigilant about maintaining continuously open lines of communication with community partners. As Devi Miron and Barbara Moely (2006) found in a recent study with 40 site coordinators of community agencies, community partners who felt that they had a voice in the design of service-learning projects reported more agency benefits as a result of the projects than those with less involvement. They also found that community partners' positive perceptions of agency benefits were correlated with a positive perception of the university as a whole. As faculty and administrators moving into a platform of eLearning, it is imperative that we include our partners' voices in this time of transition.

COLLABORATIVE REFLECTION AND RECOMMENDATIONS

The team members involved in this chapter collectively agreed that *service-eLearning* is no longer an option—it is a reality of today's educational environment. Just as eLearning has penetrated pubic and private organizational environments, it has become a key component of teaching and learning systems in colleges and universities. Based on the review conducted for this chapter, there are a number of keys to moving forward with *service-eLearning*.

First, every member of the service-learning team must be viewed and treated as an equal partner.[3] This can be most clearly demonstrated through effective communication with all partners. *Service-eLearning* has the potential to reduce disparities and communication barriers, as community partners who are physically located in different geographical locations become accessible (ideally) at the same level as the students and faculty members. An electronic platform may well assist in the perceptual and actual leveling of partner access and contribution equality. Second, *service-eLearning* practitioners should engage in a continuous review of the extant literature in education, technology, and service-learning. We have much to learn from each other, as was demonstrated in a short-term yet salient way for the members of this review team. Third, institutional support for *service-eLearning* should not only be thoughtful but also systematic in terms of the intra-campus support and external support for community partners. Fourth, to effectively understand how the inclusion of *service-eLearning* is transforming our educational ecosystems, we must actively and effectively engage in research related to personality and value characteristics of involved members (faculty, students, and community partner representatives) as well as comparisons of pre- and post-experience data comparing traditional and *service-eLearning* contexts. Fifth, as part of this examination and assessment process, the scholarship of service-learning should continue to focus on both how-to anecdotal descriptions of online trials and adaptations as well as empirical analyses and outcome data. Finally, all involved in this collective and collaborative educational transformation should remain focused on persistence, receptivity to change, and patience.

As Gerry Barnard (2005) posited, "Learners only flourish if education adapts successfully to the needs and demands of the age" (p. 24). Our primary role as *service-eLearning* practitioners and partners is to continue to create learning environments within which we, our students, and our community partners can flourish. In our increasingly technology-oriented educational environment, *service-eLearning* presents us with a new educational platform—a platform that provides us with our greatest challenges for today and our greatest opportunities for tomorrow.

NOTES

1. The articles were not ranked within each member's list, rather each list is presented in chronological order by publication date.
2. I would like to thank two very important contributors to this article, Asa L. Kenworthy, for his community partner perspective, and Jenna A. McStay, for sharing her insights as a college student. I would also like to thank the editorial team for putting together this innovative and ground-breaking book as well as the editors and an anonymous reviewer for contributions that significantly improved this chapter.
3. In recognizing the importance of reflection as part of an effective learning experience (Mintz & Hesser, 1996) and the equality of our individual perspectives and contributions (Maurrasse, 2001), we recognized that we should engage in a period of reflective processing. In support of this recognition, the team engaged in reflective, open discussions of key issues and next steps. This process proved to be an important part of our team's reflective learning experience by allowing each member to more clearly identify and articulate our own thoughts as well as learn valuable information about other members' perspectives as service-learning advocates and practitioners.

CHAPTER 3

SERVICE-eLEARNING

A Burgeoning Field

Susan W. Post

"What is common to many is taken least care of, for all men have greater regard
for what is their own than for what they possess in common with others."

Aristotle wrote these words more than 2,000 years ago and yet we find them
again uncomfortably relevant in today's society, as evidenced by Robert Putnam's (2001) bestselling book, *Bowling Alone.* Putnam wrote of the preva-
lence of socially disconnected and apathetic behaviors and their impact on
civic engagement. Leaders in the service-learning movement have long recognized this detriment and have labored vigorously toward expanding this
experience-based, academically rigorous teaching method with the hopes
of reversing disengaged behavior. Over the past decade in particular, service-learning has proven its viability toward civic engagement. In fact, this
national success has launched service-learning into international waters.
Germany in recent years has followed suit with several civic engagement
service-learning pilot projects (Sliwka & Frank, 2004). The outcomes have
been nothing short of astonishing. A German student echoed comments
found in national studies: "Before service-learning we received regurgitated
text, now we get to experience it ourselves" (Sliwka & Frank, 2004, p. 13).

Service-eLearning: Educating for Citizenship, pages 23–27
Copyright © 2008 by Information Age Publishing
All rights of reproduction in any form reserved.

The student added that she would have never volunteered, but that now she immediately would do it again.

Such comments speak directly to the global sustainability of service-learning. One can only wonder, then, about the immense potential of eLearning to facilitate service-learning student collaborations across the world. To that end, this brief chapter reviews some of the current work in the burgeoning field of *service-eLearning* to lay a foundation for the contributions of this edited collection.

One of the main components of service-learning is reflection, often comprising interactive brainstorming and journal writing. Symbolically seen, reflection is the hyphen in the term "service-learning" because it connects experience with curriculum. Reflection allows the learner to cast the service experience in terms of his or her own experience, which ultimately leads to the realization of common rights and pursuits. By conceptualizing social issues in terms of individual experience, service-learning engenders within participants a sense of social responsibility.

eLearning often utilizes online forums as a vehicle to reflect on academic activities. Discussions in online contexts differ widely from face-to-face (f2f) discussions, as the written and asynchronous process allow for critical thinking and problem-solving to emerge on an extended time frame. The luxury of time affords learners the opportunity to read, process, and respond to each other (Palloff & Pratt, 1999). It has been argued that this extra time results in more in-depth discussion as writing requires more effort, more planning, and more reflection than speaking (Joinson & Buchanan, 2001; Mills, 2001). While the lack of social presence may inhibit spontaneity in some cases, this is offset by the benefit of the online course archive. eLearning components are archived in their entirety whereas f2f discussions are normally not recorded, much less transcribed, for later reflection and processing.

Barclay Hudson (2002) wrote that many learners demonstrate their enthusiasm and interest by interrupting discussions to hasten the development of discourse or ideas. This may be counterproductive not only for reflection purposes but also on retention and cognition development: "[listening] in an evaluative way, accepting or rejecting ideas presented . . . leads to fatigue and listening shortcuts so that [learners] absorb only about 30 percent of the message . . ." (Pascale & Athos, 1981, quoted in Hudson, 2002, p. 81). The preservation of dialogue gives both learners and faculty the benefit of going back and reinterpreting earlier comments or recognizing an idea that may have been otherwise lost in verbal dialogue (Mills, 2001). In *service-eLearning*, other audiences, such as community partners or researchers, may also benefit from discussion archives.

eLearning has the potential to build greater democratic understanding and civic engagement if implemented appropriately and within a civic context. To that end, Joseph Braun (2004) offered three desired outcomes: (a) an informed citizenry; (b) rights of privacy, free speech, and assembly; and (c) enlightened self-interest and civic participation. Technology-oriented citizens will find fulfillment of these principles through search engines and databases, newsgroups and listservs, learning networks and communities, and participation in civic associations.

These outcomes were realized in several of the courses funded by "Cyber-Serve Mini Grants" from the Virginia Tech Service-Learning Center; these grants provided the opportunity to integrate technology in service-learning, suggesting tremendous blending opportunities. Faculty member Sally Naylor Johnston (1999) reported that quiet or reserved students became more apt to dialogue in the online community forum and learned about each others' perspectives more rapidly. In this regard, online discussions or asynchronous communication have the potential to be far more democratic in nature than f2f exchanges, as no one person can dominate the discussion but rather everyone gets a turn to be heard. Johnston further noted that regular f2f classroom sessions were more productive after online sessions took place and that critical reflection was deepened because of the availability of discussion transcripts.

eLearning provides faculty and students more opportunities for feedback, reflection, and revision as it provides additional communicative outlets for all stakeholders involved (Bransford, Brown, & Cocking, 1999; Mills, 2001). An area that has not yet been explored but holds great promise is that of community partners joining reflective online discussions to strengthen community ties and commitment to continued civic engagement (Johnston, 1999).

Journaling is another reflective component used in traditional service-learning pedagogies to encourage learners to monitor their own progress and reactions. Journals are recognized as a mechanism for investing ongoing attention to reflective thought. Steven Mills (2001) replaced the paper-based journaling activity in his course with an electronic journal using Blackboard, a popular course management system that offers threaded discussion forums with group functions. This functionality allowed him to organize learners according to service projects and to provide each group with an online discussion forum. Rather than having learners drop off their journals for assessment at weekly intervals, Mills had the benefit of observing learners' progress daily. He noted that the daily online peer interaction helped learners better process the service experience as it occurred rather than reconstructing their observations after the experience to meet a journal deadline. This practice of composing journal entries significantly after the service experience converts what should be a reflection activity to a memory one and is a noted challenge in the literature on effective service-learning course design (Phipps, 2005). Moreover, Mills (2001) found that the labor-intensive task of handling 50 physical notebooks and deciphering the often varied nature of their penmanship was also alleviated in the electronic journal format.

A companion benefit of integrating eLearning pedagogies is the greater visibility potential for service-learning among all learners and other audiences. Elizabeth Creamer (1999) spoke of this particular outcome as generating increased interest in service-learning among faculty: showcasing participants' projects on the Internet served as direct evidence of learner and faculty engagement and also revealed a willingness to share experiences with the broader community.

Theorists have suggested that the Web represents a tremendous educational resource for learners because of its capacity for flexible, dynamic, and adaptive presentation of information leading to self-directed and active learning (Wiley & Schooler, 2001). As such, the wiki, blog, and other social software have made tremendous headlines in recent years, particularly with respect to civic and political engagement among young adults. The ability to customize a blog, for instance, toward a specific interest and in a visually appealing format has drawn a large audience. The blog features an individual, private space for reflection while remaining open to public viewing and comment. This ability to marry individual and community concerns makes this a valuable tool for pursuing *service-eLearning* outcomes. Ulises Mejias (2006) highlighted the success of this tool in an online social software class at Teachers College, Columbia University. One of the course objectives was for the students to apply their newly acquired skills to promote a social cause or project of their choice in an effort to effect social change. This objective was met when students demonstrated ownership of the assignment by identifying and subsequently contributing in a meaningful way to the social cause. This ownership aspect, which Mejias termed "issue entrepreneurship," aids in the sustainability of students' engagement in social causes.

eLearning engages learners to think beyond their own field of interest by extending classroom work to include personal responsibility and community development. Bruce Saulnier (2005) posited the need for students to understand the civic responsibility associated with being educated citizens. He quoted the words of philosopher and Berkeley alumnus Parker Palmer: "To teach is to create a space where the community of truth is practiced" (p. 81) to emphasize the interconnectedness of education, community and social change. This is particularly important in today's culture wherein greater value is often placed on personal advancement than on achieving a balance between individual and community concerns.

Douglas Schuler (2004) addressed Putnam's (2001) discussion about the diminishing of civic life in America from the perspective of the "de-skilling" of citizenry. Civic intelligence—a form of collective intelligence that can be improved when people create, share, and appropriately act on information (Schuler, 2004)—suffered as our national identity moved from citizen to consumer. Saulnier's (2005) perspective aligns with Dewey's thoughts about the use of communication and information systems; we must use today's advanced information systems and technologies to build programs and applications that effectively negotiate shared issues.

Correspondingly, Putnam (2001) asked, "How can we use the enormous potential of computer-mediated communication to make our investments in social capital more productive? How can we harness this promising technology for thickening community ties?" (p. 180). *Service-eLearning* provides one response to that question. In the combination, both service and eLearning pedagogies are enhanced through the fostering of deep intellectual exchanges about a common goal.

· PART II ·

SERVICE-eLEARNING APPLIED

CHAPTER 4

INCORPORATING TECHNOLOGY IN SERVICE-LEARNING

A Case Study of Appropriate Use

Randy Stoecker, Amy Hilgendorf, and Elizabeth Tryon

When does information technology enhance service-learning and when does it inhibit it? There are many tools in our information technology universe today, and they are insinuated in nearly every part of our lives, including our pedagogy and our volunteerism. That they do so often without our prior planning and reflection is of some concern. While technology may appear to make life easier, the question remains: Does technology make life better?

Concerns about the role of technology in pedagogy generally, let alone service-learning, are numerous. As many campuses find the increasing majority of their distance learning students are local, concerns grow that technology separates learners, rather than facilitates access to learning experiences (Carr, 2000; Minton & Willett, 2003). Add to this concerns that technology reduces interaction among learners, does not effectively police

Service-eLearning: Educating for Citizenship, pages 31–43

31

identity falsification, and does not exert effective quality control (Green-wald & Rosner, 2003; Rowe, 2004), and it becomes evident that eLearning has a lot to overcome.

If we shift to a discussion of service-learning, we encounter another set of problems. First, it is not always clear or agreed upon just what service-learning means. Here we will use the term to broadly refer to situations where students are receiving course credit for community service. We do not mean to imply that anything occurring within that definition is *good* service-learning, however; in fact, there are myriad critiques of what oc-curs inside of that definition. On one side are those who ask whether there is actual learning in service-learning, or if it is just a glorified volunteer program (Eyler & Giles, 1999). On the other side are the critics who worry that service-learning may exploit communities as free education labor, es-pecially when the service partnership is short-term and students commit to it in order to get community-sponsored training, or use the community as a personal diversity experience, without providing any useful service (Eby, 1998; Martin et al., 2007; Sandy & Holland, 2006).

Is the combination of eLearning and service-learning, then, a disaster in the making? To answer that question, we must address the complex inter-section between technology, pedagogy, and community service.

INTERSECTIONS: TECHNOLOGY, PEDAGOGY, AND COMMUNITY ENGAGEMENT

To understand the interaction of technology, pedagogy and community en-gagement, we must actually look at the combinations created by the use of technology in both pedagogy and in service-learning. Both pedagogy and service can be conducted in a way that is completely free of technology, fully mediated by technology—where all information and communication are accomplished by technology rather than face-to-face (f2f)—or assisted by technology, where only some information and communication are me-diated by technology. There could be, for example, a course that is con-ducted entirely via the Internet (fully online) but where the service is con-ducted completely f2f in a community partner office (Strait & Sauer, 2004). The opposite is also possible, where the course is taught f2f in a classroom, but students perform the service entirely through email and the Internet, such as where students construct a webpage for an organization (Bjork & Schwartz, 2005; Malvey & Hamby, 2005).

Thus at the two extremes are the traditional service-learning course, where all the pedagogy and all the service are conducted f2f, and the eLearning approach, where all communication is conducted by phone, email, webchat or videoconference. In the middle of this continuum we find *service-eLearning*, a combination of both pedagogical approaches. Traditional service-learning, where both pedagogy and service are free of technology, may not be the best choice for meeting community needs. For example, an organization asking a student to update its paper membership files may be better served by an electronic database, and the professor may be better able to supervise the student's design of that database by viewing the system online. *Service-eLearning*, while not prescribing a fixed instructional medium or modality, instead lets the curriculum and service partnerships determine the best pedagogical blend.

Situations where much of the interaction still occurs f2f, but where technology augments communication and information management, can be called hybrid. Students meeting f2f in a classroom, but also contributing to an online forum, are engaged in a hybrid pedagogy. Likewise, students working in a community organization office, but creating a website or electronic database for the organization, are engaged in hybrid service, mediated by technology. There are, in this broad gray area between fully f2f and fully online forms of pedagogy and service, innumerable options and combinations for *service-eLearning*.

Deciding when and how to deploy technology in either pedagogy or service, then, invokes a discussion of the issue of appropriate use. When is it appropriate to use technology and when is it not appropriate? How do we decide? We are beginning to see various combinations of eLearning pedagogies and service-learning, such as the examples above, but we lack a discussion of the principles that should guide their use. This is all the more important when we consider that, when we talk about technology, we are actually talking about information and communication technologies, or ICTs (Stillman & Stoecker, 2005). ICTs involve both information management and communication management. The interaction of these two issues and their associated technologies (including everything from digital cameras to cell phones to the computers they both interface with) can get quite complicated. It may be that some kinds of information are best communicated in one way and other kinds of information in another way. This chapter is an initial attempt at developing principles to guide the appropriate use of ICTs in the combination of pedagogy and service, and of face-to-face and online instructional mediums.

A CASE STUDY OF COMMUNITY-BASED RESEARCH

We address the issue of appropriate use of technology in service-learning through a case study of one form of service-learning called community-based research (CBR). While community-based research, or CBR, can be done with or without students, in its service-learning form CBR involves students conducting research that is guided by community-generated questions, with community-informed research methods, and supporting an action agenda (Strand et al., 2003).

CBR can be viewed as an enhanced form of service-learning because it is more community-directed than the typical curriculum-driven service-learning approach that can emphasize student learning over community impact (Strand et al., 2003). In addition, the connection between the service and the learning is typically tighter in CBR than in traditional service-learning. In CBR it is very clear how the research project is helping to build the students' research skills. In service-learning it is often unclear how serving soup, for example, enhances one's understanding of poverty (Eyler & Giles, 1999), or helps to eradicate it.

We report here on a unique example of CBR, which utilized a *service-eLearning* approach. First, it employed several technology tools to make the project go more smoothly. Second, the project was actually an evaluation of *service-eLearning*. Our CBR project is probably best described as a *service-eLearning* pedagogy with f2f service. We tried to also use a hybrid service process, mediated by technology, but, as we will show, our community partners did not respond enthusiastically to our use of technology and even consciously opposed it at some points.

Early Project Development

Responding to feedback from community organizations about the challenge of dealing with large numbers of University of Wisconsin-Madison[1] students requesting service-learning placements around the city, a focus group was organized with approximately two dozen community organizations in fall of 2005 that confirmed those concerns, and produced a core group of seven nonprofit agency leaders to guide a CBR project documenting service-learning from the community's perspective. From the inception of the project, appropriate use of technology was an issue. For example, the course description was sent via email to recruit students; however, the vast majority of the fifteen seminar students, including two co-authors of this chapter, signed up as a result of the professor's visits to other courses and then through word of mouth.

It was clear that the project would be a significant undertaking, with more than 100 small and medium-size nonprofit organizations in or near the city hosting service-learners. The core group, students, and instructors agreed that an in-depth interview methodology would be the best way to learn about community reactions to CBR. We realized such a method would produce a huge amount of data. In addition, the collaborative research design process would require significant time and quick review of drafts to finish the project in one semester. Considering these issues, the professor created an online content management system for the course.[2]

We then set up monthly meetings with the core group and students to design the research, decide how to present it, and organize a community event for it. Based on past experience we surmised that simple email announcements would not suffice to get the core group members to meetings (which we confirmed a few months later when we temporarily stopped phone recruitment). Here again, the superficial efficiency of information technology would have created inefficiencies had we relied on it solely.

The Project Seminar

The course was offered through the Department of Sociology, but students came from various disciplines, drawn by interests in action-oriented research and community involvement. Most were graduate students, but undergraduate and special students, including AmeriCorps*VISTA members, also joined the class. The class met weekly, and the community organization core group met with the students monthly during class sessions at a community center.

Preparing to do Research

The professor adopted the roles of project manager, trainer, and guide for the students and community-based organizations alike, rather than expert or lecturer. We focused early on establishing expectations and forming a base of student understanding, front-loading the course with preparatory readings and activities to ensure ample time for completing the research project.

We held the second class meeting at a nearby community center with the core group representatives, where together we identified key issues for our research, consciously using a "low-tech" device, the flip-chart. We have found that participants contribute more when they can see their words being written down. The lists filled an entire wall of a large community activity room and included issues such as organizations' experience with service-learning, relationships with the higher education institution, training service-learners, characteristics of service-learners, managing service-learning in the organization, and service-learning outcomes. Organization representatives also shared thoughts on the most appropriate methods for recruiting participants and gathering data.

The students and the professor used the content management system early on in the *service-eLearning* experience to negotiate the course contract, including student requirements and grading procedures. We also created a database of local small to medium-sized nonprofits that had experience with service-learning in some form. Students used the content management system forum to reflect on readings about CBR methods and ethical issues, qualitative methods, and service-learning. In online discussions, students grappled with how to address service-learning issues in ways that would be both achievable and significant. The professor used the file-sharing features to post a draft interview protocol and then refine it with student input.

Other aspects of the *service-eLearning* project were not appropriate for hybrid, technology-mediated processes such as an activity for student training in interviewing skills. Interviewing, when done well, is fluid, responsive, and essentially social, an art as well as science, particularly in community-based research (Dick, 2000). Especially when done with community workers who operate in a f2f culture, this kind of partnership requires a f2f process. To prepare, students completed readings and viewed an online lecture on in-depth interview techniques, then trained in two class meetings; one of these reunited the students with the core group for practice interviews. Students interviewed the core group representatives using the protocol and then debriefed the experience. We did not completely neglect technology in this portion of the *service-eLearning* experience, using the content management system to post notes from the debriefing and to further refine the protocol.

Collecting the Data

We continued to emphasize f2f interaction during the data collection stage of the project, though with some important technology enhancements. Each student called or emailed the directors or volunteer coordinators of five or six local community-based organizations to request an interview, using the online database of organizations where they could quickly determine which organizations had not yet been chosen by others. They also reviewed the organization's website to enter the interview with some basic knowledge.

Students took extensive notes in addition to recording all interviews with a digital recorder. After each interview, students typed and uploaded a partial transcript, along with the original recording, to the website and phone calls were also used to confirm facts. We discovered too late that the recorders were not compatible with Macintosh computers, requiring those students to bring their recorders to the professor to upload recordings through his computer, introducing some inefficiency into the process. The value of uploading the recordings themselves is questionable. We intended that all students could use the repository to listen to all the recordings, but they relied mostly on the transcripts. However, the process did create an important central data archive that was backed up off-site. It is important to note that all of the transcripts and recordings were protected both through username/password access to the content management system, and file access was restricted to only usernames of each of the course members.

The online forum served an important function at this point in the research project. Many students were new to interviewing and transcribing and sought support and guidance from their classmates on the forum. The forum allowed students to address data analysis issues as they arose, rather than waiting for the next class meeting, provided a venue for students to raise questions to the professor during his out of town travels.

Analyzing the Data

The data analysis process relied heavily on technology mediation, as we had interview data from sixty-seven community organization representative interviews—each averaging an hour in length.

We conducted the analysis using a grounded theory (Glaser & Strauss, 1967) research process and an adaptation of the wiki information management process (Carpenter & Roberts, 2006) that complement each other effectively. Grounded theory builds theoretical findings from continuous comparison of multiple data sources. Wikis are web-based collaboration tools that build knowledge through continuous revision by multiple authors. The most famous of these is Wikipedia, an online encyclopedia authored by volunteers who contribute and edit entries. The belief is that continuous review and editing by a large number of people will produce the most accurate information. We did not use formal wiki software, but the draft sharing on the website during the analysis stage was very similar to a wiki process.

We began the analysis in class, as students shared interview experiences and began to identify themes from the data. The process then shifted to the website. Students downloaded the partial transcripts from the website and reviewed the texts, confirming and adding to the themes discussed in class. The professor posted his ideas on the emerging themes on the forum and had students react to them. Students compared the themes to their interviews and suggested changes. For example, one student found that, in discussing their motivation for hosting service-learners, some interviewees saw service-learning as providing extra hands to keep the organization running, while others viewed service-learning as an obligation for them to prepare future nonprofit professionals. Another student distinguished these discussions as "self versus altruistic motives" or "organization versus student benefits" and believed that the organization's orientation greatly influenced their subsequent decision-making about such things as accepting student service-learners and evaluating their work. Because of this discussion we reframed a theme on service-learning definitions to highlight organizations' motivations and goals for service-learning as well. This technology-enhanced process allowed seven themes to iteratively emerge: goals and motivations of community organizations finding and selecting service-learners; the structure of *service-eLearning* projects; project management; diversity issues; relationships and communication with the higher education institutions; and indicators of success.

Students then divided into pairs (to further analyze each theme). Some divided the transcripts for individuals to analyze and others had all group members analyze all transcripts. In reviewing the transcripts again, students identified information and quotes that referred to the themes and constructed a number of sub-themes. Some of this work was done in class or through email; however, most groups decided to also meet outside of class time. One group met in a local coffee shop with wireless access, so that each member could bring his or her laptop to download and upload work immediately from and to the course website.

The groups shared their sub-theme analysis in class and on the course forum, which further clarified and confirmed our themes and helped identify connections across themes. Much of this dialogue took place over email or the course website.

The Research Report and Action

Each team took responsibility for crafting the findings from their theme into a chapter of the report for the community organizations. As with analyzing the data and identifying themes, technology allowed groups the flexibility to take various approaches toward the collaborative work, depending on their individual schedules and preferences. Some groups worked back and forth through email, and some worked f2f abetted by laptop computers.

The course forum again assisted in this process. Writing a report with multiple themes and fifteen different authors is a very challenging task. Our primary objective was a simple, comprehensible report for the community organizations to learn of our findings. Some students requested general guidelines for formatting and overall style. Students also used the forum to negotiate the best use of particular quotes and ideas that cut across themes, and decide what to call the research participants (e.g., "respondents," "interviewees," or "nonprofit staff?").

As groups completed their drafts, they posted them to the course website. The professor did general editing to identify overlaps among the pieces and to address other minor issues to ensure a comprehensible report for the community organizations. The authors of this chapter are continuing to refine the drafts for further dissemination.

Community Partner Reactions to Technology

The service component of CBR requires that the research supports action. So we planned a celebration event, with the guidance of the community organization core group, to motivate the action phase of the project. In this phase we shifted away from technology. Even before we finished our analyses, we began to discuss our ideas for the event in class meetings and on the course forum. Then, when we asked the core group how we should present our findings at the event, one core group member shouted out "No PowerPoints!" followed by nods around the room. Their argument was that PowerPoint reinforced one-direction communication and passive learning and they wanted an interactive event. So instead we designed a poster session to share the research findings, "fishbowl" discussions highlighting best practices in *service-eLearning*, time for networking and resource sharing; and small group planning sessions for using the research results to suggest ways of improving service-learning.

Each small group transformed their theme from an outline or report form to a poster format that would encourage interaction between the student researchers and the community organizations. In contrast to a typical PowerPoint presentation, students used the posters to both convey the major findings of their sub-theme and to create interest and spur questioning, and most included anonymous quotes from the interviews to illustrate the findings. Some of the more technologically-savvy groups used Adobe Illustrator or a similar program to create their posters; others used word processors and affixed sections to the posterboard. All groups also prepared accompanying handouts of their themes for the community organizations to take with them.

The poster session was central to the event. Each group of students stood near their posterboard to answer questions about their theme as organization representatives circulated and read the board contents. The participants were given notes with adhesive backing to place on the posterboard that outlined the topic they were most interested in delving into in small-group discussions. Following the posterboard discussions we then held two "fishbowl" discussions where students re-interviewed nonprofit staff members who seemed to have the most developed service-learning models. Finally, we divided participants into the small group planning discussions based on where they put their notes. When these discussions began, the community organization staff contributed recommendations centering on the sub-themes labeled on each posterboard. There was overlap in recommendations across the groups, with the greatest overlap around a need for some sort of "community standards" document that detailed the needs of the organizations in working with service-learners. The event proved an invaluable networking opportunity, leading to several future university–community partnerships.

Post-Seminar Implementation

One of the greatest challenges in CBR is putting the research into action. We again employed the CMS to create a public website (Stoecker, 2007) to post the results of the students' research and the community planning sessions. As we were invited to present the research results at various conferences (which we turned into workshops), we posted the workshop results as well.[3]

DISCUSSION: LESSONS ON APPROPRIATE USE OF TECHNOLOGY IN SERVICE-eLEARNING

What have we learned about the appropriate use of technology in this project? There are six important lessons.

1. **Technology Encourages Deeper Analysis.**   Because we could all so easily access each other's writing online, there was significant engagement at different stages of the research process. The content management system, coupled with an online forum, was very effective in developing the research design and interview guide, and in conducting the data analysis. Students sifted and winnowed through the data again and again and shifted back and forth between varying opinions and perceptions. People could access any draft at any time, as well as the transcripts on which the draft was based, and post their comments. Particularly since we had to spend so much class time just on the logistics of the project, the content management system was sometimes the only way that we could conduct the depth of analysis the material required.

2. **Technology Encourages Discussion.**   One of the concerns expressed by students was that there was not enough time available in class to process the experience through reflection. The tension in service-learning between meeting the students' educational needs and the community's practical needs was evident in the seminar, and the professor's emphasis was on making sure the community project got completed with quality results. Consequently, much of the f2f class time was spent on project logistics rather than the deeper philosophical and theoretical issues the project was raising. Here the forum became very important, as it provided a space for students to discuss those deeper issues. Issues surrounding race were particularly important in the class, and one of the most active forum threads involved a discussion of how race was important in the complex relationship between mostly white service-learners, mostly white community organization staff, and communities of color.

3. **Technology Supports Long-Distance Communication.**   Because professor involvement was one of the requirements most strongly supported by our community organizations, the content management system and email allowed for efficient communication and was an adequate substi-

tute for the lack of f2f contact. Due to extensive travel of the professor, for a brief period the seminar operated similar to a distance learning course where all interaction with the professor was electronic, though the students continued to meet in small groups. It is important to note, however, that one of the reasons a temporary distance education process may have worked was that we had already built f2f relationships, which we are learning is also true of our relationships with the community organizations.

4. **Technology Produces Information Efficiency.** In this project we needed to share sixty-seven transcripts across as many as fifteen people, distribute drafts for quick response, and solve problems throughout the research process. By putting everything online in an organized electronic folder system, we attained amazing information efficiency. This is especially important in a project designed to serve community organizations within one semester. Of course, achieving these results required the technology to operate seamlessly. In the one case where it did not, as we discovered that our digital recorders would not interface with Macintosh computers, it was quite frustrating for the students involved who had to trek over to the professor's office on the far end of campus to have him upload the interviews.

5. **A Flexible Approach to Technology Maximizes its Benefits.** One of the most important things we learned is to be flexible in response to differing levels of comfort with technology. Some students did all their editing online, never printing out a page. Others printed out everything and did all their work on hard copy. Some students were very comfortable using the forum and email, and others really needed to meet f2f. In a project requiring such a high degree of cooperation, it was essential to have technology support that allowed everyone to play to their strength. The content management system was new territory for most class members, and some experienced a degree of trepidation when first approaching the concept of uploading audio files, downloading interview transcripts, and generally interacting in concert with fourteen other people over cyberspace without mistrust in the infallibility of the system or just worrying about getting files confused.

It is also clear that the value of technology changes during the course of a project, and it is crucial to be sensitive to its costs and benefits. By listening closely to the nonprofit core group, we were able to temper our use of technology and limit its application to the aspects of the project where it would do the most good. We took notes on flip charts during meetings with the core group rather than using a laptop and projector, since nonprofit staff were much more familiar with flip charts. Digital technology was especially helpful, indeed crucial, during the analysis stage of the project, but not so much during the data collection and reflection stages.

6. **Technology is not a Panacea, Particularly with Community Organizations.** While electronic communication worked well for the seminar participants, it did not work as well with the community organizations. In many cases, the nonprofit staffs' work revolved around f2f communication, and they saw email as an alienating form of communication. As students made follow-up calls to the staff that were sent emails, the staff often admitted to "having seen something in my inbox but I haven't read it yet," or denied having gotten anything. Organization email addresses also change frequently as staff change jobs or organizations restructure. Then we have to start from scratch to orient new staff contacts to the project, which requires relationship development that cannot be done well through email. Another indication of nonprofit staffs' reluctance toward technology was our core group's preference for poster boards rather than PowerPoint presentations at the community event. Organizing the community event around poster boards got people up and talking, rather than sitting passively watching slides, and it supported the nonprofit f2f culture. It may be that technology becomes more appropriate once f2f relationships are well established. It is important that whatever technology used be extremely user friendly, stable, and secure.

GUIDING QUESTIONS

Although CBR is much more information-intensive than the typical service-learning projects, and information technology can consequently play a much more clearly defined role, we believe the lessons we have learned in this project can provide a general set of questions that service-learning designers can use in determining the extent to which they want either the pedagogical or service components of *service-eLearning* courses to be technology mediated. These questions are:

1. What do we know about both the student and community partner preferences and capacity for working with information technology?
2. What efficiencies and inefficiencies might technology introduce into the project?
3. In what ways could technology inhibit or encourage deeper student reflection and thinking?
4. In what ways could technology inhibit or encourage interaction?

Asking these questions will help lead *service-eLearning* projects to appropriate use of technology, rather than simple avoidance or unreflective adoption.

NOTES

1. The authors wish to thank the University of Wisconsin Morgridge Center for Public Service for a small grant supporting the seminar on which this chapter is based, and anonymous reviewers for comments on an earlier draft.

2. A "content management system" differs from the traditional online course management software in that it is more oriented to file sharing and information management by an entire group, rather than primarily by a professor. The new content management systems have advanced well beyond the collaborative web model described by Andreas Dieberger and Mark Guzdial (2003), which were often just collective file storage spaces. Today's content management systems allow users to post content and interact around it and revise it in real time. The University's existing course management software was not flexible enough to accommodate our need for a collaborative online environment emphasizing file sharing. The professor manages a department-based server, and installed the e107 (2007) content management system on the server to handle the course. While not as extensive as Drupal (2007) and not as well known as content systems such as Wordpress (2007), e107 is an extremely stable system that is very easy to install. It includes easily-configured file storage and sharing, online forums, posting, and address management, which we used extensively.

3. Underscoring the need for this type of technology-mediated university–community collaboration, the final outcome of this project is a draft book manuscript based on the research results. The seminar students are now spread across the globe. A core of us (including the authors of this chapter) is now revising the pieces and will soon be posting them for review by the original authors. Here, again, email and an online content management system are proving beneficial, as the original authors can see our revisions and respond to them as they choose.

CHAPTER 5

CONSTRUCTING EXPERIENTIAL LEARNING FOR ONLINE COURSES

Two Models of Service-eLearning

Jean Strait

As eLearning has grown exponentially in use and popularity, educators are dramatically increasing their use of online learning technologies and formats within constructivist pedagogical principles. Faculty and learners are viewed as active co-participants in the learning process. Faculty are repositioned as mentors and guides instead of the "all-knowing" authorities often associated with traditional face-to-face (f2f) pedagogies. In the last few years, in particular, advances in technology and online connectivity have been driving forces in educational reform across modalities. An emerging phenomenon is the development of new educational paradigms for online education. Unexplored issues and challenges have materialized from these new paradigms, prompting investigation of several issues related to quality in online instruction:

- Effectiveness of online learning versus f2f instruction.
- Collaboration and cooperation of students.

Service-eLearning: Educating for Citizenship, pages 45–58
Copyright © 2008 by Information Age Publishing
All rights of reproduction in any form reserved.

- Types of student interactions.
- Training and professional enhancement for faculty.
- Planning and implementation of curriculum delivery.

Interactions, both teacher-to-student and student-to-student, are essential to success in the online environment. To be successful, instructors are examining ways to not only foster these interactions within the online classroom but also to engage students in their local communities through experiential learning opportunities. Experiential education is a general term to describe academically-related work experience (Giles, Honnet, & Migliore, 1991). Experiential education includes such activities as internships, practica, cooperative learning, student teaching, and service-learning that bridge learning in the classroom and learning on the job. In addition to nurturing and supporting responsive eLearning environments, experiential learning components strongly influence the types of interactions students and teachers have with each other. Experiential learning online courses is an excellent way for students to gain the experience their f2f counterparts receive by virtue of regular in-person contact with faculty, fellow students, and community partners.

SERVICE-LEARNING IN ONLINE COURSES

In addition to preparing students academically, institutions of higher education are being called upon to prepare students for the complex issues in the workplace. Students are often successful in academic content but lack the skills needed to be successful on the job (Jacoby, 1996). Over the last decade, colleges and universities have turned to service-learning in response. Service-learning is a form of experiential education in which students engage in activities that address human and community needs together with structured opportunities intentionally designed to promote student learning and development (Gelmon et al., 2001, p. 20). By structuring experiential learning opportunities that promote student learning through engagement in the community, service-learning fosters students' critical thinking and interpersonal skills. Students participating in service-learning:

- provide community service as a part of their academic coursework;
- learn about and reflect upon the community context in which the service is provided;
- develop an understanding of the connection between service and their academic work (Gelmon et al., 2001).

As higher education incorporates more and more fully online and hybrid course offerings, a critical challenge emerges to develop experiences for online students that provide workplace exposure and engage them as community members. Conventionally, service-learning projects are structured in a local community, usually in proximity to the higher education institution where students can easily gain access. In an online course context, however, students are based in their own local communities, which may not be the same county, state, or even country where the higher education institution is physically located. The challenge then, is how to provide a quality experience in service-learning while meeting the needs of multiple students in multiple communities.

CREATING AN ONLINE SERVICE-eLEARNING MODEL: THE FIRST GENERATION

Bemidji State University (BSU), a mid-size state university in Minnesota, offers a teacher education program known as DLiTE, or Distributed Learning in Teacher Education. DLiTE is a Desire2Learn-enhanced teacher education preparation program that serves the state of Minnesota. Currently, BSU enrolls 5,000 students from 40 states and 44 countries and offers 98 undergraduate programs of study, including 13 pre-professional programs. However, it is important to note at the outset that neither the f2f education program nor the DLiTE model are NCATE accredited programs and follow their own placement guidelines.

Responding to the shortage of teachers in the United States, BSU, the Minnesota Satellite and Technology Center, in partnership with The Perpich Center for Arts Education, The Walker Art Center, the Paramount Theater and Visual Arts Center, and Anoka-Ramsey, North Hennepin, Central Lakes, Century College, Fergus Falls, Inver Hills, Itasca, Lake Superior, Normandale, Rainey River, Ridgewater and Rochester Community Colleges have developed a blended-technologies, K–8 Elementary Education program for rural and urban students who, for various reasons, cannot attend a campus-based teacher education program.

By using what is already available in terms of courses, professors, organizational structures and student support services and technology, this program allows for a flexible development and delivery system to accommodate future growth and technology enhancements. The DLiTE cohort program launched for the first time in the fall of 2002. Each cohort contained 25–30 students. In this program, *service-eLearning* replaced the traditional field placement and practia experiences of the f2f model.

Features of the program include:

- Weekend f2f classroom experiences with professors for two times per semester. These meetings take place at the Perpich Center for Arts Education (Minneapolis), the Paramount Theater (St. Cloud), or Bemidji State University (BSU).
- Student-selected teacher-mentors who work exclusively—in real classroom settings—with one-on-one time for students and mentors.
- Online classroom using WebCT, BSU's instructional management system.
- eMentoring by faculty through WebCT, e-mail, telephone, and interactive television, as needed.

Service-eLearning in DLiTE

Students in the DLiTE model had service-learning attached to their online courses beginning in their second semester and have at least one course with a service-learning experience each concurrent semester thereafter. Pedagogy, Language Arts I, Language Arts III, and Science methods all infuse *service-eLearning* in their coursework. A description of one such infusion follows.

Language Arts I

For the first class in the language arts sequence, the professor utilized eLearning to facilitate methodologies for teaching reading to elementary school students. Since the students were distributed throughout the state, each of them had individual *service-eLearning* placements which they helped arrange. Students volunteered with summer school programs, worked with local libraries, contacted local youth organizations and provided additional support to community centers. Each student learned about a particular methodology, applied it in the service-learning placement, and reflected on the nature of the experience in their online classrooms. Students were required to complete 10 hours of service-learning as a major component of the course. The community organization received services by having the students work on their individual needs.

For example, one student contacted the local library, which also doubles as the elementary school library in the community. The student completed a needs-assessment for the library and determined that the elementary science trade books were not being requested. She then created a system to "introduce" new books to the children by creating bulletin boards featuring these science stories. The librarian reported to the *service-eLearning* student that requests for the books sharply increased so much that demand out-paced supply. The success of the student's instruction and bulletin boards increased the use of the science books by approximately 500% in two months. This same student then created a guide for parents to help them determine how to help their children make appropriate reading selections. The library staff estimated that the local community's use of the library escalated dramatically, with approximately 45% more books being checked out than in the previous six months combined.

In another example, a student worked one-to-one with a struggling reader in second grade for 12 weeks. Based on the student's analysis of the child's vocabulary development and comprehension levels, tested at the end of the twelve weeks, the child improved in vocabulary by 35% (as compared to a 12% average for peer improvement) and comprehension by 43% (as compared to a 5% average for peer improvement).

Monitoring, conducting, and reflection on the service-learning experience was all handled electronically. Students were required to follow a format for planning and implementing, which was sent weekly to the professor along with a log of what experiences were taking place, how long each lasted, and what impact was experienced by the student for that day. Students were engaged in reflection through journaling, discussion boards, group projects and final summative reflection pieces. Within the context of the final summative piece, several of the students reported through reflection that the *service-eLearning* component was the most valuable experience they had to date working with children and learning how to use community resources. One student reflected:

> This service-learning experience has been a positive spin on my teaching and Tony's reading and reading comprehension. Going into education classes I assumed I will learn an abundance of theories, skills, information, and strategies that I can use in my future teaching. However, up to this point there has not been a time when I could learn the skills and strategies and directly applied what I have learned to how to teach it. This has been one of the most beneficial projects I have been given up to this point in my education. The most exciting part of this project is the success I believe it has brought to my student.

The community partners were similarly enthusiastic because they were not required to invest additional training in the DLiTE students since they were already receiving that training through coursework. Community partners benefitted from the extra help (especially with shrinking budgets) so much that they began sending regular requests for *service-eLearning* projects and students.

THE HAMLINE UNIVERSITY MODEL: THE NEXT GENERATION OF SERVICE-eLEARNING

Hamline University is a high-quality, nationally ranked, comprehensive university with more than 4,000 students in its undergraduate college, law school, and graduate schools. Ranked first in quality and value among comprehensive universities in Minnesota by U.S. News and World Report magazine, Hamline University's mission is "to create a diverse and collaborative community of learners dedicated to the development of students' knowledge, values, and skills for successful lives of leadership, scholarship, and service" ("About Hamline," 2007, para. 2). Unlike BSU, Hamline University's Education Programs are NCATE accredited and reviewed by the Minnesota Department of Education every five years. In addition, the online learning platform used at Hamline University is Blackboard, and although it is similar to Desire2Learn, its form and function have been reported by students as easier to use.

At Hamline University, both online and f2f courses can be offered by the same instructor. This made it easy to create a model using educational psychology courses taught by the same instructor. As courses reported here were designed, it was important to determine what skills to measure in pre-service teacher development. The next step was determining if service-learning would indeed promote the intended skills.

Service-Learning and Skill Acquisition

Janet Eyler and Dwight E. Giles (1997) called for future research which utilizes a variety of methodological approaches to shed further light on the efficacy of service-learning in producing its intended outcomes. Jeffrey Anderson (1998) pointed out some of the intended outcomes of service-learning in teacher education which include to:

1. foster an increased awareness and acceptance of cultural diversity;
2. promote problem solving;
3. encourage critical thinking and meta cognition;
4. further personal development and self-esteem;
5. assist teacher efficiency;
6. provide for moral development;
7. cultivate civic attitudes and levels of citizenship (also see Westheimer & Kahne, 2003)
8. facilitate leadership skills and team work;
9. enhance content knowledge gains (also see Shastri, 1999);
10. expansion of community awareness;

11. relationship building;
12. practice and reflect on decision making;
13. enhance learner concept development (see also Strait, 1994)
14. self awareness of strategies (see also Strait, 1994).

Maria Elena Galvez-Martin, Connie Bowman and Margaret Morrison (1996) indicated that when pre-service teachers engage in reflective activities, they improve their level of reflection but do not achieve the highest levels of reflection without specific training. But what are the levels of reflection, and how do teacher educators train pre-service teachers to progress through those levels? To complicate this further, how do practitioners capture all the components of service-learning and show student growth over time?

Theoretical Framework and Methodology for Hamline University Model

Often, pre-service teachers do not get the opportunity to reflect on decision-making. The goal of reflection is to appraise the teaching/learning situation as a whole so that one can make decisions in the classroom that are pedagogically appropriate, ethical, and just. Initially, pre-service teacher reflections were simply retelling, with little or no interpretation or analysis, what the events they experienced actually meant. Experience levels make the difference. The pre-service teachers with extensive experience and well-integrated service-learning tended to approach the social problems related to their service in a more complex and thorough way and were more likely to have well-developed strategies for citizenship action than those with limited experience (Eyler et al., 1997).

Jean Strait (1994) examined reflective thought through portfolio entries for an adult developmental reading class in which three levels of reflective thought were present. The first, the defining level, was evident in students trying reflection for the first time. Enculturated with the system of schooling, this level was marked by comments of immediacy, teacher direction, dependency on grade assignment, and group dynamics. Many students operating in this level transitioned to the next level only after a significant amount of relational trust was built between them and the instructor. The second level was the critical thinking level in which students could identify strengths and weaknesses, began to take risks and experiment. Students were reflecting on how they learned and considered new ways to look at the world around them. Students still could not correct ineffective strategies but they could at least identify those strategies. In the final level, the metacognitive level, students were developing an awareness of the different strategies they were using and began to use more than one strategy. They attempted to correct ineffective strategies, and developed an awareness of a general knowledge base that guided them in the selection of strategies to use and the implementation of those strategies. Strait's (1994) developmental levels exemplify Stephen Brookfield's (1987) definition of critical thinking, which states that being a critical thinker is part of what it means to be a developed person, and fostering critical thinking is crucial to creating and maintaining a healthy democracy.

The Hamline University Model sought to use the research base on teaching skills as put forth by Anderson (1998); link them to the reflective levels presented in Strait (1994); and then compare the student reflective comments made by examining the comments from both a f2f class and online class. The instructor was the same for both courses. A rubric was created to measure these skills as evidenced in student's reflective work. Students' comments were coded by both skill and reflective levels (see Appendix, Table 5.1).

Conclusions from Hamline University Rubric Study

Once the student comments were coded and analyzed several differences emerged:

1. Both sets of students easily commented on their K–12 students' skill level but had great difficulty discussing their own skill level as preservice teachers.
2. F2f students had more comments about immediacy issues.
3. F2f class was more articulate in explaining how they applied content knowledge from the course information.
4. Community awareness appeared in more online course reflections (12% vs. 3%).
5. Online students outperformed the f2f students service hours by a 2–1 ratio (40–60 hours vs. 20 hours). Also, more than 35% of these same students stayed on in the placement after the semester was complete.
6. Some rubric category comments were barely visible (all below 4%): Levels of citizenship, Diversity, Group dynamics, and Decision making.

Why could some of these low percentages have occurred? Teacher interaction on these topics may have played a role in the low level of responses. Little whole-group discussion was done in the areas of citizenship development, diversity development, and decision making. Replicating this study and having more class discussions and interactions on these three skill areas may increase the amount of comments coded in these areas. Self-awareness of strategies and application of content knowledge were stressed heavily in both classes, and both showed much higher percentages. Another concern this brings to light is the possibility that students were responding as they think the professor wanted them to, saying what they think the professor "wanted." If certain topics were not stressed, it follows then that they simply were not addressed in the reflective pieces because students did not see them as valuable. Also, it can be argued that online education attracts a different kind of student, usually non-traditional, with work experience, and who can more clearly articulate their ideas.

Challenges

With the BSU model of *service-eLearning*, the largest challenge was determining how one university professor can manage all the individual *service-eLearning* projects that students are doing. In the Hamline University *service-eLearning* setting, one instructor can manage a course group by using one community partner for the entire group. Twenty-five students at one site can make a greater short-term impact for the community partner and are easier to direct when they are all working on the same project. The challenge of partnerships can also be a benefit. When students are working with multiple projects, they can tailor their *service-eLearning* to their own major interest. When students are motivated by personal interest, learning and retention soar. Also, multiple community partners benefit from the varied *service-eLearning* projects.

Because online students tend to be non-traditional ages and usually work a 40-hour week in addition to going to school, access to a community partner can be a challenge. University professors need to do their homework to provide a list of potential partners. By providing potential choices and targeting county and state agencies, students have a better chance for connecting with a long-term community partner.

Finally, reflection can be a challenge for students. Most students are familiar with keeping a log of hours or writing short papers about their service-learning experiences. To determine how the *service-eLearning* are impacting the students, deeper levels of reflection are required. This means the university professor needs to provide more opportunities for discussion, and assign more reflective-type activities for the students completing the *service-eLearning*. Instructors must specify and give examples of various stages of reflective comments. This takes time for the students and the instructor. In addition, using pre and post surveys and questionnaires can and will help to further distinguish growth in students from beginning to end of semester.

SUGGESTIONS FOR FUTURE SERVICE-eLEARNING MODELS

When considering the development of a *service-eLearning* component for online courses, several lessons can be applied from the BSU and Hamline University models.

Lessons Learned

Start Small. It is important to remember that online learning is new for many faculty. They need time to create and need to be reminded to start with one class and work out all the details for that *before* they start with other courses.

Train the Students. Teach students about service-learning, *service-eLearning*, community partnerships and reflection as a part of the course content. This can begin with a *service-eLearning* information section visible to students on the course home page. This tells them the details—who, what, when, where and why—the nuts and bolts of service-learning. Then the instructor can create a discussion room where students can discuss ideas for their *service-eLearning* projects. Finally, in the assignments section of the course, have students post their completed project plan. This way, students can view other students' ideas as they build their own projects.

Plan for Community Partner Contact. Find a way for community partners to contact faculty. It may be through email or phone. Having a handbook for the students and community partners assists in determining the role of each in the *service-eLearning* relationship. Creating an online area for discussion of community partners can link similar organizations throughout the state. Community partners want to be sure they are providing the best experiences for students. Faculty must keep an open door.

Plan Extra Time for Unexpected Outcomes. Often, when students begin eLearning, they are not quite sure what to do and how to do it. This takes discussion time from student-to-student and teacher-to-student. Build in time for experimentation and revision of their service projects.

Include a Reflection Component. Do not forget to have a reflection piece so students can look at their *service-eLearning* experiences in depth. Students need time to process what they are learning and how to apply that learning to future situations. Students also benefit from direct instruction in effective reflection practices.

REFLECTION: THE VALUE OF SERVICE-eLEARNING

When conducting online courses, *service-eLearning* is an excellent outreach to community organizations. As the educational paradigm shifts from f2f to more online formats, students and communities will be looking for ways to gain work experience and build long-lasting partnerships that will be used in their future careers. The experiences provide rich, authentic, hands-on training for students. eLearning challenges students to think in new ways, explore new ways of problem solving, and raise critical questions about their learning and service. *Service-eLearning* enhances student academic experience through experiential learning and these valuable experiences reflect the complex issues of students' future workplaces. Students get the opportunity to wrestle with complex issues right in their own communities and to become a part of the solution. These solutions are shared with peers statewide, assisting other small towns and businesses that may have similar needs.

The introduction of *service-eLearning* at institutions of higher learning is an ideal method to create a bridge between academic learning and community service. It gives individuals a chance to share knowledge and learn more about how to use each methodology while connecting with community partners and their needs. Students can also potentially build long-lasting community partnerships that they will use when they enter their profession full-time.

Student learning is enhanced by providing multiple opportunities for practice and reflection. To date, examples such as journals, discussion boards, presentations, group projects and one-on-one discussion with the professor serve as the tools of reflection. This same reflection is valuable to guide students as they address community concerns. Students add to the richness of the dialogue by influencing the direction the dialogue will flow, sorting key ideas for deeper discussion and focusing on key points. The *service-eLearning* experiences allow students to not only sharpen the focus of their own instruction and learning but to deepen the level of inquiry through questioning, making connections, and honoring multiple perspectives.

NOTES

1. Portions of this chapter draw upon content used with permission from the 2004 article "Constructing Experiential Learning for On-line Courses: The Birth of E-service" by Jean Strait and Timothy Sauer published by *Educause Quarterly*.

2. Currently, a study is in process at Hamline University where college students are paired with grades 4, 5, and 6 classrooms. The first college rubric has been modified and is being implemented. In addition a 4/5/6 student rubric model is being used to follow elementary students through a three-year project. All students self-assess pre and post through the civic action scale, a sub-component of the Civic Attitudes and Skills Questionnaire (CASQ). Results of the first year of the study are being analyzed and will be available fall 2007. The three-year project will conclude June 2010. A second project is being designed which will use *service-eLearning* to pair United States and South African pre-service teachers through the use of *Internet2*. The project is expected to launch fall 2007. Students will have local community partners and will share experiences and information with pre-service counterparts across the ocean.

APPENDIX

TABLE 5.1   Levels of Reflection for Assessing Service-Learning (© Jean Strait 2003)

Student skills	Stage 1 Defining Level	Stage 2 Critical Thinking Level	Stage 3 Metacognitive Level
Learner concept development	Definition of self as learner	Asking for examples and samples	Creating examples and samples to reinforce their ideas/beliefs
Self-awareness of strategies	Definition of course goals. Unclear of personal strategies strengths and weaknesses	Identifying strengths and weaknesses in current strategies and methods	Identifying and improving ineffective strategies
Understanding of service-learning	Definition of process of service learning	Identifying issues within the service-learning context	Continuing to work on issues after the service-learning placement has ended
Application of content knowledge	Immediacy issues— what is due right now? Not able to see the big picture or long-term goals. Time confines the reflective process. Dependency on grade assignments	Considering new ways of looking at the world around them. Beginning to consider larger issues and greater impact. Experimenting with new ways of learning	Can articulate the broader issues, larger context and discuss their role in their world. Sees service as one way to contribute to society. Completing self-directed tasks to improve environment of service-learning placement

Student skills	Stage 1 Defining Level	Stage 2 Critical Thinking Level	Stage 3 Metacognitive Level
Diversity development	Defining diversity— what does it mean in the community?	Investigating new communities and both personal and group attitudes about communities	Self-confidence and comfort in communities different from the students cultural identification
Learning format	Teacher direct instruction and influence	Teacher guided practice Scaffolding	Explaining the process of student self-thought
Group dynamics	Defining group dynamics What roles do they take? What do they do about conflict? • How do they do negotiations within the group?	Students show evidence of group negotiations and affirmations of individual's experiences in service-learning	Empowered to actively defend independent ideas/ thoughts/beliefs
Levels of Citizenship	Personally responsible citizen—one who acts responsibly in his or her community by volunteering, donating, and obeying laws	Participatory citizen- actively participates in the civic affairs and social life of the community at the local, state, and national level- they recognize the importance of planning and participating in organized efforts to care for those in need or to guide policies.	Justice-oriented citizen-calls explicit attention to matters of injustice and to the importance of pursuing social justice. Seek to improve society by critically analyzing and addressing social issues and injustices to effect systemic change.
Moral development	Students focus on self-interest	Students make choices about moral reasoning based on commitment to specific individuals and relationships	Students morality based on the principles of responsibility and care for all people.
Problem-solving	Students are unclear of problem(s) or solution(s)	Students have identified problem(s) but are unclear of solution(s)	Students are clear on problem(s) and solution(s) and actively engage in solution

(continued)

TABLE 5.1   Levels of Reflection for Assessing Service-Learning (© Jean Strait 2003) (continued)

Student skills	Stage 1 Defining Level	Stage 2 Critical Thinking Level	Stage 3 Metacognitive Level
Relationship building	Students are placed with community partner and interact with community partner on a regular basis throughout the length of the course	Students identify and build upon relationships within the community organization and with individuals	Students maintain a relationship with the community partner after the service-learning placement has ended
Community awareness	Background knowledge of community issues	Can identify needs, problems, strengths and resources of community partner	Relates community issues with larger social issues and actively brings about change and growth in the community
Decision making	Preactive-planning for decision-making before the placement begins	Interactive-actual decision-making while in process—"on your feet" decisions	Post active-evaluative reflection—making decisions about changes or adaptations after the placement has ended

CHAPTER 6

HOW DISCUSSION BOARDS DRIVE COURSE CONCEPT MASTERY IN SERVICE-eLEARNING

Kristine F. Hoover, Maureen Casile, and Ralph Hanke

According to John Dewey (1916), reflection is a purposeful effort to explore and consider the relationships between actions and outcomes. Critical to the service-learning process is student reflection on how the service experience applies to course material (Godfrey et al., 2005; Silcox, 1995). Service-learning projects without a commitment to reflection risk becoming an effort of volunteerism rather than a pedagogical tool (Eyler & Giles, 1997). In work by Dale Blyth, Rebecca Saito, and Tom Berkas (1997), students indicated a reduced sense of responsibility toward civic involvement and serving others when reflection was not present. Reflective activities in service-learning are most beneficial when they are a result of clear objectives and goals for students learning from the service experience; enable students to make a real contribution to individuals they are serving; encourage students to participate actively in their own learning; help students develop a sense of community; are both structured and flexible, reflexively

Service-eLearning: Educating for Citizenship, pages 59–73

relate classroom learning to out-of-class experience; are engaging and on-going; and use a variety of methods to respond to different learning styles and abilities (Cairn & Kielsmeier, 1991).

The reflection process can require extensive in-class time for introspection and discussion, placing time demands on course instructors because of the need for feedback. This additional effort can make service-learning seem both daunting and overly time-consuming. The use of eLearning pedagogies for team discussion, reflection, and feedback can address both of these concerns. Specifically, discussion boards can serve as an effective tool for facilitating the feedback process at both the individual and team level. This chapter explores one facet of the integration of eLearning and service-learning pedagogies: The use of online discussion boards as tools for reflective writing and as sources of collaborative learning and peer feedback.

SERVICE-eLEARNING VIA DISCUSSION BOARDS

Online Learners. A growing body of research indicates that students both appreciate and benefit from eLearning via discussion boards. For online learners, discussion boards can alleviate isolation by building mutual support within the community for both the task and the learners (O'Reilly & Newton, 2002). Discussion boards can also facilitate collaborative learning among dispersed populations of learners (Curtis & Lawson, 2001). Online learners have complained, however, that discussion board interaction can be time-consuming (Meyer, 2003; O'Reilly & Newton, 2002), particularly when other participants are slow to respond or provide incomplete information or feedback (Curtis & Lawson, 2001; Vonderwell, 2002).

Face-to-Face (f2f) Learners. Although it is useful to understand the benefits and limitations of discussion boards in online learning, considerably less is known about the role that a discussion board might play in a hybrid setting, where face-to-face (f2f) interaction is available. This distinction is important for three reasons. First, studies of discussion board use in online courses have measured the degree to which the discussion board can serve as a substitute for f2f discussion, especially when the latter are not available. However, it would be useful to know whether the discussion board adds value in ways that complement or augment what f2f interactions can offer. Second, studies of online classes are limited to subjects who have self-selected into a learning environment with minimal f2f interaction. These learners may differ in important ways from students who opt for the traditional classroom (Dutton, Dutton, & Perry, 2002). Finally, much of the work in discussion boards involves graduate-level classes and classes of relatively small size. Selma Vonderwell (2002), for example, working with a class size of 22, was able to respond to student emails within 48 hours and post weekly feedback to the whole class and to each student. This level of instructor support is desirable given that students tend to dislike "too much compulsory discussion that is not structured" (O'Reilly & Newton, 2002, p. 466). Nevertheless, it may not be pragmatic in larger classes with multiple large sections all managed by one instructor. This gives rise to the question of whether a discussion board can facilitate learning in settings where instructor feedback and support are limited and less individualized attention is available than in an online or small class setting.

The present chapter seeks to expand on existing research in several important ways. Most notably, this chapter seeks to measure the contribution of eLearning via discussion board to acquisition and mastery of fundamental course concepts within in a service-learning course. Presuming that eLearning can facilitate the kind of reflective interaction that service-learning requires, we explore the ways that eLearning uniquely complements service-learning. Our experiences confirm discussion boards as a primary vehicle for linking the pedagogies of eLearning and service-learning and suggest guidelines for integrating these approaches.

Group Dynamics and Service-Learning Aims

Researchers have long argued that learning is highly contextual and socially constructed and is therefore an outcome of the reciprocal determination process among personal characteristics, environmental influences, and one's behavior within a given context (Bandura, 1977; Kolb, 1984; Senge & Scharmer, 2001). One type of learning context is collaborative, team-based learning and it has been shown to be an effective method to increase student achievement at many grade levels. For example, various formats of cooperative learning programs, such as Students Teams-Achievement Division (STAD; see Slavin, 1986), Team Assisted Individualization (TAI; see Slavin, 1985), and Cooperative Integrated Reading and Composition (CIRC; see Stevens et al., 1986), apply the principles of cooperative learning to instruction in reading, writing, and language arts to enhance students' learning.

It is our position that team learning and collaboration foster service-learning aims in the following ways. Collaborative learning brings motivational benefits to students by enhancing their persistence following failure to solve a problem. Research has found that this type of persistence resulted in an increase in both the number and difficulty of additional problems students attempted, as well as the overall level of individual learning (Lan & Repman, 1995). Therefore, we argue that team learning facilitates selecting, designing, implementing, and evaluating service-learning projects. In addition, team learning carried out on electronic discussion boards provides a forum where students can constantly re-evaluate their service-learning opportunity and the procedures required to implement high levels of community service.

Gary Kleinman, Philip Siegel, and Claire Eckstein (2002) showed that working in teams engaged in a variety of auditing and consulting activities significantly improved individual levels of learning. There is also evidence showing that exchanging ideas in teams with specific, realistic tasks can increase individual level learning. For example, Robert Slavin (1983) found that when teams engaged in specific tasks as opposed to simply studying together, group level rewards substantially increased individual level learning. Our experience has shown that team learning helps students prepare for all aspects of their service work by helping them develop a clear understanding of the task, the skills, and information required to complete the task, awareness of safety precautions, and knowledge about and sensitivity to the specific contexts of a given service-learning project.

Further, an extensive meta-analysis on the effects of social context (i.e., small group vs. individual learning) indicates that, on average, small group learning had significantly more positive effects than individual learning on student achievement (Lou, Abrami, & d'Apollonia, 2001). Finally, a study that examined 49 teams involved in management simulations showed that the more realistic the simulation the more effective the individual level learning (Adobor & Daneshfar, 2006). Therefore, based on our research into social and collaborative learning, we offer that team learning promotes service-learning by encouraging communication and interaction among students as well as reflection before, during, and after service provision and encourages the use of multiple methods to encourage the critical thinking that is central in the design and fulfillment of service-learning outcomes and curricular objectives.

We argue that learning teams operating in an eLearning environment are better able to engage in service-learning by encouraging students to work in a more reflective fashion, to listen better, to open up, to share their perspectives, and to invite feedback. Given that, service-learning activities value diversity in participants, practice, and outcomes and encourage partnerships and collaboration with the community, electronic discussion boards serve as a vehicle for improved team learning by providing a safe environment (O'Reilly & Newton, 2002) for students to engage in discourse on course concepts, which, in turn, prepares the students for engaging in the activities required to succeed in service-learning projects.

Therefore, students engaged in team-based, applied service-learning projects—especially those where the interchange of material that relates to the content of the course is stressed in an online environment—are very likely to exhibit a stronger ability to both function in the service-learning environment and individually retain class materials than students who study individually using only lectures and textbooks as a source of information.

SERVICE-eLEARNING IN A MANAGEMENT COURSE

We integrated eLearning into three sections of a f2f service-learning course, "Principles of Organization and Management." The course is a required course for non-business juniors and seniors who come from 17 different degree granting programs at a mid-sized state university. The programs ranged from applied health science to visual communications technology. A total of 56 students, 22 female and 34 males with virtually none classified as "traditional" (e.g., born prior to 1980), participated in our investigation into the value of eLearning as a complement to learning gains in a service-learning course.

Consistent with the goals of civic engagement and corporate social responsibility, management students benefit from a greater understanding of the environment in which their future clients and customers live and their future employees and businesses operate. As a means of understanding the needs of the greater community, the service-learning project for this class required students to become more involved with constituents they may not have met otherwise.

Service-learning teams were given the responsibility of researching and then coming to consensus on a client of their choice for their service-learning project. They were instructed to come to agreement with the client on how to best meet the client's needs. All projects had to provide two hundred units of service as defined and agreed upon by the student group and client organization. Once the teams completed a proposal, it was submitted to the instructor for approval.

The student teams worked independently outside of the class to complete their service-learning project. Two class periods were allotted for collaborative work time during the semester and one week (three class periods) was allotted at the end of the semester for presentations to classmates and clients. In addition to the initial written proposal submitted at the beginning of the project, each team was also required to submit a final written document summarizing their experiences and outcomes.

In all, 12 service-learning projects were completed during the semester. Clients ranged from The Foundation for Hospital Art to the United States military. Students' contributions ranged from blood drive outreach efforts to communications with seniors through the creation of greeting cards that would be distributed throughout the upcoming year. Specifically, The Foundation for Hospital Art is a nonprofit organization that provided preprinted canvases and paint supplies to a student team for one of the service-learning projects. According to The Foundation for Hospital Art (2003), their mission is "to give comfort and hope to those who suffer in hospitals by providing artwork at no cost to hospitals" (para. 1). The team of five college students enlisted more than 200 additional members of the campus community to not only complete three paintings, each of which was approximately six feet by six feet in size, but also to personally sign one of 200 greeting cards for patients that included an image of the painting that was being sent to the hospital. In completing this project, the students viewed a video and learned about the importance of aesthetics to the healing process. Another example of a completed service-learning project involved a team working with teachers at a local elementary school prior to Veterans Day to develop a teaching unit on military service. To do this, the college students had to research and create the material to present to the elementary students. The college students presented the information to several classes of fifth grade students and the fifth grade students then responded to the information by creating more than 200 letters and cards for the soldiers. The college students then reviewed and sent the letters to the military organization with which they had made previous arrangements.

Discussion Board Pedagogy.   Using the discussion board, "group pages" were set up so that team members could easily communicate with each other. During the implementation period for the project, each individual team member was required to post or "add a new thread" a minimum of four times. Ideally, these postings were to be completed at a minimum of once per week over the five-week implementation period. The course content was divided chronologically into several separate sections: introduction, planning, organizing, leading and controlling. Students were to reflect on how the material from each section applied to their service-learning experience. Within each reflective writing post, students were instructed to use a bold font to emphasize any and all course terminology used. No maximum number of postings was set; there was no limit on the number of course terms that could be used in any single posting; and students were free to use terms repetitively.

In addition, students were to "reply" a minimum of four times to various team members' postings throughout the project. Replies were to indicate more than a superficial reading of the team members' thoughts: Replies were to integrate new course concepts, clarify questions asked in the posting, or expand the posting with other related course material. There were no points awarded specifically for discussion board participation or quality.

The instructor's role during the posting process was to respond to any questions that could not be resolved within the group and to provide greater clarification upon request. The instructor was not an active contributing member of each group's discussion board. At the end of the semester, all members in a group received the same grade for the project. However, individuals' grades for the project could be influenced positively or negatively based on feedback from group members regarding an individual's level of contribution.

In this f2f setting, working with 56 student participants, eLearning enabled the critical reflection process that would not have otherwise been manageable. Using the discussion board, students could share ideas and receive feedback from group members asynchronously to accommodate various scheduling requirements and communication styles. For the study, total quantity of course concepts on the discussion board was measured by total course terminology used in reflection, including terms used on more than one occasion. Breadth of course concepts was measured by unduplicated terminology used in reflective writings. The students were not given explicit instructions on quantity or breadth or terminology to be used in each reflection. The discussion board reflection posts were presented to the students as a required component of the project. The students were made aware that the material in the discussion board postings could provide a foundation for their final presentations and final written documents. Again, there were no specific points awarded for participation or quality of the discussion board reflections, however, the discussion board could provide objective data as a means of confirming a student's level of engagement. Team members had the option of dismissing underperforming members if they so chose.

The management concepts addressed in the course were organization theory, objectives, policies, decision-making, authority, management development, leadership, communication, motivation, effective human relations, and management principles. Relative to course material in the reflective writings, it was not uncommon for students to apply concepts such as the Job Characteristics Model and intrinsic motivation when they felt a sense of meaningfulness, responsibility, and had actual knowledge of the results of their service-learning projects (Hackman & Oldham, 1980). They commonly wrote about the five-stage model of group development (Tuckman, 1977), as their teams "formed, stormed, normed, performed, and adjourned." In addition, they better understood the importance of goal setting (Locke, 1968) and clear expectations through the expectancy model (Vroom, 1964) and could tangibly see how individual differences impact behavior in their service-learning projects. All of these concepts and many others were covered in the text and then brought to life through eLearning, peer learning, and ultimately *service-eLearning*.

Overall, projects were assessed on two criteria: Application of course material and client satisfaction. A rubric was used to measure application of course material in the proposal, class presentation and final written document. Clients were asked for feedback by the instructor via email, phone, and/or hard copy regarding the students' professionalism and attainment of agreed upon goals.

At the end of the semester, students were presented the opportunity to participate in a research study. Participation would require them to complete a survey, for which, they would receive extra credit in the course. The survey contained two sections, one that assessed content mastery and a second to obtain demographic and attitudinal data. The twenty-four content mastery questions were multiple choice questions taken from the text publisher's test banks. One knowledge-based and one application-based question were selected from each of the chapters covered in the course. Students were not given any advance indication that the survey would be a "test" of their mastery of course material.

MEASURING STUDENT LEARNING OUTCOMES

Upon undertaking this inquiry, we assumed that the total quantity of course concepts that individual students used to reflect upon their *service-eLearning* experience in an eLearning environment will be positively correlated to content mastery, as would the breath of course concepts. We held the same assumption regarding collaborative reflection via discussion boards: the cumulative total quantity of course concepts would be positively correlated to mastery of course concepts by individual members of that team. These hypotheses were tested using simple correlations between measures of discussion board usage and content mastery. Results are summarized in Table 6.1.

This analysis showed a positive correlation between the number of references to course concepts in discussion board posts and content mastery, and between the breadth of concepts referenced on the discussion board and content mastery. Overall, these findings indicate that discussion board usage, even repetitive usage of the same terms, improves content mastery. Our second hypothesis, however, was not supported as no significant relationship was found between the number of references to course concepts made by an entire group and the content mastery of individuals in that group.

TABLE 6.1   Discussion Board Usage and Content Mastery

(n = 56)	Score	Correlation	p <
Content mastery	73.64	N/A	N/A
Discussion board usage	29.8	0.36	0.01
Discussion board breadth	21.2	0.29	0.05
Group discussion board usage	150	0.14	N.S.

Note: N.S. = Not Significant; N/A = Not Applicable. All correlations are with content mastery.

Gendered Dynamics and Discussion Board Usage

A surprising and significant result of our research dealt with differences based on gender. Table 6.2 indicates that while men and women did not perform differently in terms of discussion board usage or content mastery, their attitudes toward discussion board usage differed in a number of ways. Women generally viewed the discussion board more favorably and reported that it helped them:

- get work done,
- gain better insight and understanding into their service-learning and experience,
- communicate effectively with the instructor.

TABLE 6.2   Gender Differences: Performance

	Women	Men	*T*	*p* <
N	22	34		
Course performance	75.73	71	1.42	N.S.
Content mastery	76.05	72.09	0.95	N.S.
Discussion board usage	32	29	0.55	N.S.
Discussion board breadth	23.4	19.9	1.17	N.S.

Note: N.S. = Not Significant

TABLE 6.3   Gender Differences: Attitudes

	Women	Men	*T*	*p* <
N	22	34		
Discussion board helped to:				
Get work done	1.42	2.04	−2.91	.01
Gain insight into the service-learning experience	1.70	2.18	−2.84	.05
Communicate effectively with instructor	1.78	2.63	−2.59	.05
Willingness to rely on eLearning technology to contact the full group:				
Discussion board	30.74	19.16	1.82	.10
email	21.69	14.23	2.00	.05
F2f meetings out of class.	19.45	34.88	−2.97	.01
Willingness to rely on eLearning technology to contact a subset of the full group:				
Discussion board	23.86	12.80	1.86	.10

TABLE 6.4 Gender Differences: Correlation of eLearning Usage with Content Mastery

	Women	Men	T	p <
Correlation (Usage and Mastery)	0.50		2.57	0.05
Correlation (Usage and Mastery)		0.27	1.55	N.S.
Correlation (Breadth and Mastery)	0.54		2.91	0.01
Correlation (Breadth and Mastery)		0.14	0.83	N.S.

Note: N.S. = Not Significant

In addition, women expressed a greater willingness to rely upon threaded electronic communication than did their male counterparts. In self-reported measures, women were more likely than men to use the discussion board and email to communicate with the full group while men were more likely to rely upon group meetings outside of class. Women were also more likely than men to use the discussion board to contact some subset of the full group.

Based on these self-reports by subjects, the data was divided into men (N = 34) and women (N = 22). Results are summarized in Table 6.4.

For men, the correlations between discussion board usage and content mastery and between breadth of concepts in discussion board usage and content mastery were both insignificant. On the other hand, both were significant for women. Moreover, a regression of the number of references to course concepts in discussion board posts on content mastery for women showed that the number of references to course concepts in discussion board posts explained 23.6% of the variance in content mastery.

MOVING FORWARD WITH DISCUSSION-BOARD FACILITATED SERVICE-eLEARNING

While mastery of course content is hardly the only goal of service-learning, it is, nonetheless, an important goal. Evidence that *service-eLearning* can improve content mastery would be particularly of interest to the instructor who may fear sacrificing valuable class time and other resources to an enterprise based solely on the building of character or citizenship. This research adds to a small but growing body that shows that service-learning can improve content mastery if students are required to reflect upon their service-learning experience and how it relates to course concepts. This research further shows that, at least for some students in some settings, eLearning pedagogy and technology can reduce the amount of class time, and perhaps total time spent coordinating service-learning experiences and reflections so as to make these feasible for a wide variety of courses.

Although students do not always care for required threaded discussions with minimal moderation by the instructor, the results of this study indicate that these discussions are associated with content mastery in a service-learning environment. This study showed no correlation between content mastery and exposure to the reflections of others, even others with whom the student is working closely on a service-learning project. Rather, it appears to be the student's own reflection, both on his or her own experiences and on the utterances of teammates, that is associated with content mastery.

These findings do not necessarily negate the potential contribution of teamwork to learning in a service-learning environment. However, they do indicate that the value in teamwork may be more in the doing than in the reflecting. It is also possible that interaction via discussion board may contribute to content mastery in some context other than required reflection as part of a graded assignment—for example, if teammates were joint problem-solving via discussion board. Although beyond the scope of this study, this would be a worthwhile area for future study.

Gender differences in the relationship between discussion board usage and content mastery were a surprising finding worthy of further exploration in discussions about *service-eLearning*. These findings may well indicate that women who choose to reflect deeply and broadly on course concepts on a discussion board are rewarded with greater content mastery than less reflective women. For men, greater use of the discussion board for reflection does not appear to have a payoff in terms of content mastery. Furthermore, based on their responses to attitudinal and behavioral questions, the subjects of the study seem to know this.

These findings are somewhat surprising in view of a number of studies that indicate men enjoy a greater power advantage in asynchronous computer-mediated communication (see Herring, 2001). Specifically, Susan Herring (2001) reported that men tend to dominate asynchronous computer-mediated communication by verbal intimidation (Kramarae & Taylor, 1993) as well as more subtle types of dominant behavior (Herring, 1992, 1993). These behaviors create an adversarial environment from which women tend to shy away (Herring, 1992). There is also evidence that women enjoy a significant advantage over men in decoding the kinds of nonverbal cues that would come to them only in f2f encounters (Blanck, 1981). So it seems counterintuitive that women would favor a mode of communication that denies them this advantage.

One possible explanation for these findings may be a tendency by gender to prefer one format to another. It is possible, for example, that women are more likely than men to favor the time for reflection offered by a threaded discussion while men tend to favor the quick resolution of f2f problem-solving. On the other hand, it may be the task itself—reflection—that serves women better than men in terms of concept mastery. What these results indicate is that men are mastering course concepts as well as women, but reflection via a discussion board is not the mechanism by which they are doing it. Perhaps it is via reflection in another forum or perhaps it is by some activity other than reflection. It would be advisable for future studies to investigate preference for reflection versus spontaneity to see if this is a driving force behind what we noted as gender differences.

The question of discussion board reflection and learning in men is one that merits further study and refinement. We do not recommend tailoring service-learning assignments by gender based on these results or any others given that differences within gender can be very great even for traits and behaviors generally accepted as gender specific. We should also consider that having reflective threaded discussions available through eLearning in a class where f2f discussion is also available, may be leveling the playing field for women rather than putting them at an advantage. Once again, men and women performed the same on a test of content mastery and on exams throughout the course. However, if additional research fails to show learning for men as a result of this activity, then it may be worthwhile to ask if there are other ways to structure service-learning experiences and reflections so that both men and women utilize their time and learning resources efficiently and effectively.

How satisfaction or dissatisfaction with eLearning influenced student attitudes toward a service-learning project in general is difficult to say. It is noteworthy that when asked about the service-learning experience in general, women were more likely than men to report that the service-learning experience helped them learn and grow as an individual and to retain what they had learned. They were also more likely than men to report that they had performed up to their potential. This may be related to greater comfort with reflection via eLearning technology, or it may be some other factor. For example, women reported slightly more volunteer work in the years just prior to taking the class. So they may have started out with a greater sense of confidence in their ability to do this kind of project than the men did.

OPPORTUNITIES FOR FUTURE EXPLORATION

Having found that discussion board reflection may influence male learning differently than female learning, it would be useful to look into areas beyond the scope of this study, perhaps even using a case study analysis. Specifically:

1. This research makes a case for a causal relationship between threaded discussion via discussion board and content mastery, at least for women. Our research shows correlation between the two in a situation where the discussion preceded measurement of content mastery. This research did not rule out all possible alternative explanations for the correlation. It is possible, for example, that higher intelligence caused both greater content mastery and increased use of the discussion board. This study did not factor in intelligence as a control variable. It is noteworthy, however, that if intelligence did drive both discussion board usage and content mastery, it did so only in women and not significantly in men. The men in this study performed about the same in the course and on the content mastery survey as did the women. One might infer from these outcomes that the men in this study were about as intelligent as the women in the study were. Men also used the discussion board about as much as women did. What differs between the two is only the correlation between discussion board usage and content mastery. This makes the alternative explanation of intelligence as a driver of both discussion board usage and content mastery seem somewhat implausible, although not impossible.

2. In this study, we didn't measure reference to course concepts in f2f discussions. This may be where men are achieving mastery of course concepts comparable to that of women, or they may be doing so independent of any group reflective activity. One means by which this might be determined would be to design a study in which group meetings are video-recorded and later coded for references by individuals to course concepts. This data could then be added to the discussion board reflections data.

3. In this study, we did not capture data on individual learning styles. Variations relative to multiple intelligences, personality, and ethnicity are likely to influence student preference to reflect alone or in a group, through writing or by more artistic means. Future research on the use of electronic discussion boards for reflection should include these moderating variables in the analysis.

4. This study did not distinguish between discussion board contributions that were highly insightful and those that appeared designed simply to meet the course requirements. It is possible that higher quality contributions offer more to learning than those that simply go through the motions. On the other hand, if minimal contributions to meet a course requirement were found to have an effect comparable to that of well-crafted contributions, then this too would be an interesting finding, lending support to the practice of com-

pelling discussion board participation even for students who do so reluctantly.

5. Timing of postings was self-determined by the students and not controlled for by the instructor. It would seem likely that there would be an effect on content mastery if postings were made throughout the service project (before, during, and after the project) versus posts made en-masse at the end of the project. Further studies should be designed to measure the effect of the timing of the postings.

6. There was no way to determine how closely each student was reading the posts of others. It may be that, contrary to the findings of this study, group posts do contribute to group member learning when the student carefully reads and considers those posts. Unfortunately, this study was not designed to provide such a refined analysis of discussion board usage. Data collection in this study was limited to discussion board usage for purposes of reflecting on course concepts as they related to the service-learning experience. No data were collected on discussion board usage for group coordination and problem solving. However, given that women were significantly more likely than men to see the discussion board as helping them get work done and communicating with the instructor, it may be useful to revisit the more utilitarian postings on the discussion board to see if men and women are using it differently for these tasks.

7. Students, and women in particular, seemed to use eLearning technology for command and control of the project as well as for reflection. It would be useful in future studies to see how eLearning influences students' ability to efficiently organize themselves and their work. This is yet another way in which eLearning technology might make service-learning feasible for a wide range of courses.

In conclusion, it was found that, for women, reflection on discussion boards strongly influenced the level of personal mastery of the course material. It should also be noted that women seemed aware of the efficacy of this approach both reporting satisfaction with and interest in using discussion boards as a vehicle of communication. What remains unanswered is why women would prefer this approach and find it more useful than men. Nevertheless, it is important to note that providing women with an additional vehicle for communicating course concepts is a powerful tool for increasing women's mastery of course material while not undermining men's ability to learn. Therefore, we recommend that course instruction at the university level integrate additional vehicles for discussing course materials, such as discussion boards to increase the efficacy of instruction, especially for women.

NOTE

The authors would like to acknowledge and thank graduate assistant Ryan Holley for his hard work to helping analyze the data for this study.

CHAPTER 7

SERVICE-eLEARNING AND PROFESSIONAL WRITING

Sandra Hill and Christopher Harris

Without face-to-face (f2f) interaction, where expressions and a handshake work to forge bonds and mend fences, young professionals in the increasingly e-linked work environment must be keenly aware of practicing good citizenship and respect for others by keeping at the forefront common goals. E-linked job environments, with their diverse work participants and modes of engagement, offer special challenges to teachers of professional writing. How can we prepare students for this kind of writing environment?

Service-eLearning (defined here as service-learning projects conducted online) can be a venue for teaching students the kinds of citizenship skills and online writing skills that can help transition them to electronic professional environments. Service-learning has proven pedagogical value in helping students learn course skills and develop community relationships and social skills, including skills in cooperation and tolerance (Eyler & Giles, 1999; Huckin, 1997; Jacoby, 1996). According to a six-year study on service-learning by Janet Eyler and Dwight E. Giles (1999), "[s]ervice-learning is a predictor of tolerance over the course of a semester when service-learning students are compared with those who do not participate" (p. 54). Because service-learning projects take students outside of the classroom, the poten-

Service-eLearning: Educating for Citizenship, pages 75–85
Copyright © 2008 by Information Age Publishing
All rights of reproduction in any form reserved.

tial for direct translation of civic and technical skills to professional life may be increased.

Service-learning has particular value for technical writing instruction. Thomas Huckin (1997) wrote that service-learning offers technical writing pedagogy both "better writing skills and opportunities for civic education" (p. 57). Scholarship on the pedagogy of online service-learning, however, is limited. Lacking is a methodology for teaching and managing service-learning projects in the environment of online professional and technical writing classes.[1] Students enrolled in online programs should have the same opportunities for civic and professional engagement as traditional students. Since "[e]-service enhances student academic experiences through experiential learning that reflects the complex issues of students' future workplaces," it is important to develop *service-eLearning* pedagogies (Strait & Sauer, 2004, p. 64).

This chapter combines the theory and practice of service-learning with that of online learning to create a *service-eLearning* paradigm for a technical and professional writing course. The practices can be applied to a fully online teaching environment or to a hybrid one. We draw upon research and our experience to show how a reciprocal relationship between service-learning and online learning can be adapted to *service-eLearning* in a professional writing class. After defining service-learning and discussing its value, we present a plan for linking assignments that can accommodate a *service-eLearning* project. We then present methods of writing and managing the project using an online course portal.

SERVICE-eLEARNING AND TECHNICAL WRITING PEDAGOGIES

In a technical writing class, service-learning projects can include any kind of document production for a nonprofit or service organization, from recruitment brochures to informational PowerPoint presentations to annual reports, manuals and instructions. Students practice the skills they are learning in the course, such as document design, clear and concise language use, and utilization of graphics, in putting together a document that will be used by the community partner. For example, students might produce a brochure for recruiting high school students to be big brother and big sister volunteers for their local Big Brothers/Big Sisters chapter. Students might create an informational PowerPoint presentation to use for training new Red Cross volunteers at their local Red Cross chapter. They could write public relations articles about university needs, such as help with controlling litter or instigating recycling, to submit to the local newspaper for sponsorship from individuals or organizations. Both types of outreach and communication accomplish much to unite town and gown.

The theoretical rationale for service-learning in professional education is well established. In their book *Educating Citizens: Preparing America's Undergraduates for Lives of Moral and Civic Responsibility*, scholars Anne Colby, Thomas Ehrlich, Elizabeth Beaumont, and Jason Stephens (2003) recognized that "a morally and civically responsible individual recognizes himself or herself as a member of a larger social fabric and therefore considers social problems to be at least partly his or her own" (p. 17). This concept of seeing oneself as part of a larger, social entity is crucial for workers of today in the global work environment linked by the thread of the Internet.

Eyler and Giles' (1999) study of the effectiveness of service-learning suggested a positive impact on student learning. They found that, in a well-structured service-learning project, a majority of service-learning students say that they learn more and are more motivated in service-learning classes than in regular classes; that they have a deeper understanding of complex social issues, subject matter, and application of material to the real world; and that application of the course work, as well as opportunities to reflect on their work, is associated with more learning. Although they found that grades were not always higher in service-learning classes than in regular classes, the researchers saw the value of application of coursework to be an advantage nevertheless (p. 80). From the standpoint of personal development, the researchers found "Service-learning is a predictor of an increased sense of personal efficacy" (p. 55) among students and, as reported by the students, greater self-knowledge, spiritual growth, and satisfaction in helping others.

What is the civic rationale for service-learning in technical communication classes? Why do our future communication specialists, legal writers, and web designers, for instance, need to do service-learning? One need only think about the spate of school shootings, the debacle of Enron and World Com, and other moral and ethical dilemmas of our century to see the need for civilizing this and the next generation of professionals. In the book *The Role of Service-Learning in Educational Reform*, Robert Bhaerman, Karin Cordell, and Barbara Gomez (1998) quoted the work of V. Perrone who suggested that among society's problems today are "a youth culture that has few connections to civic life, feelings among youth of having no vital place in society, deteriorating communities, and an increased pessimism about the future" (p. 8). How can technical writing instruction address this dilemma? Cezar Ornatowski and Linn Bekins (2004) suggested in their article "What's Civic about Technical Communication? Technical Communication and the Rhetoric of 'Community,'" that the scholarship of technical writing is trying to connect the practice of technical communication "to broader democratic and human concerns" (p. 252). The "goal is to 'civil-ize' technical communication by disengaging it from its origins in, and bondage to, industrial bureaucratic practice" (p. 252). Service-learning, with its emphasis on working for the common good, might be part of the solution to the cronyism that enabled the Enron scandal. Online technical communication students need the benefit of service-learning as much as do their on-campus peers. Ornatowski and Bekins remind us of the international and virtual existence of the modern corporation: "'communities' in which business, especially corporations, are located now are international, diverse, and sometimes 'virtual'" (p. 252).

Melody Bowden and J. Blake Scott (2003) in their book *Service-Learning in Technical and Professional Communication* identified benefits specific to professional writing students, including: application of professional writing principles to non-academic situations, interactions with real-world audiences, management of major projects across time and space, and confrontation of real-world ethical problems (pp. 13–17). Their book provides a method for setting up and carrying out a semester-long service-learning project and bears out the value of this work. The students are required to manage their projects through several writing and presentation assignments (e.g., project plan, proposal, and oral presentation) across the whole of the semester. At the end of the project, students reflect on their contribution to the community and update their resumes to reflect this applied writing experience.

Our experience facilitating *service-eLearning* projects in hybrid technical communication classes at University of Louisiana at Monroe (ULM), has confirmed several practical and civic advantages including: working with diverse constituents; experiencing firsthand the need for civic engagement in one's own community; understanding the real constraints of professional documentation by working with real-world audiences; behaving more professionally by virtue of having to enter and negotiate a professional discourse community; understanding the value of cooperation with student peers; and appreciating writing and communicating with technology, its benefits and shortcomings. These experiences with diversity, cooperation, and technology can prepare students for the modern workplace.

Online learning serves a basic cultural need by making education accessible to those who hold full time jobs or do not live near colleges (Ko & Rossen, 2001). In *Remediation: Understanding New Media*, Jay David Bolter and Richard Grusin (2000) discussed technological changes that could help substantiate *service-eLearning*. "Immediacy," or the desire to access information without consciously seeing the medium in which it is presented (pp. 272–273), is achieved through remediation, the act of borrowing and combining components of different technologies to create a product that "fills a lack or repairs a part in its predecessor" (p. 60). In this way, *service-eLearning* "remediates" service-learning through its humanitarian component, which helps teach students about civic responsibility, combined with its relevant online writing experience. *Service-eLearning* in professional writing exposes students to practical writing situations that prepare young professionals for careers in business and industry.

In "The Nature of Composition Studies," Andrea Lunsford (1991) argued that "our realities and systems of knowing are not reflections or givens that are discovered ready made but rather are themselves composed" (pp. 8–9). Though Lunsford discussed college composition courses, she made a pertinent statement about the realm of education by arguing that students learn best by actively engaging and re-engaging course materials. Thus, students can more effectively learn technical writing by engaging in professional writing practices while still in the college classroom. Additionally, technology enhances education by making communication and multiple revisions more efficient because the hypertext's malleability frees students from the constraints of working with assignments written on paper (Bolter, 1991).

While working on their *service-eLearning* projects, students have the opportunity to communicate electronically with each other and with their clients. A number of online communications systems provide students with the platform to collaborate electronically. Several colleges have contracts with online course platforms such as *WebCT* and *Blackboard*. Additionally, instructors or students may opt to utilize free online communications systems, such as *Yahoo!Groups* or *Jotspot*. Most online communication systems offer the same interface tools to foster collaborative service and learning, including group pages, asynchronous discussion areas, synchronous discussion areas, personal profile pages, file servers, document storage areas, an announcement area and e-mail communication tools. In the following section, we consider how *Blackboard* can best suit *service-eLearning* projects, which utilize five primary assignments: a justification memo, a formal proposal, the service document itself, a progress report, and reflection.

MODELS FOR SERVICE-eLEARNING PROJECTS

Setting Up Assignments and Securing Service-eLearning Partners

In an online *service-eLearning* project, students can begin their work with online research of nonprofit community organizations in need of documents. When the students find a potential client to work with, they then form interest groups around those organizations and begin the online professional communication, with a query email asking the agency if it has any documentation needs and if it is interested in working with the class to fulfill those needs (see section on "electronic mail" below). After the initial contact is made and feedback is secured, the students may continue to communicate online through email with these organizations to iron out a preliminary agreement on what the students can and cannot do for that agency in the line of documentation service.

Linking Assignments

Assignments pertaining to the *service-eLearning* project can be linked across the semester. This procedure allows the students to engage the process of project work and document production as it is done in the workplace. The first formal written communication is the *justification or recommendation memo,* in which the student team (by this time the students are functioning as temporary interest teams) presents to the potential *service-eLearning* client the rationale for their project (usually the one the team has discussed with the client in their email correspondence) for that organization. After the teams get an email acceptance in response to their memo, they form final teams of interest around the organizations that responded positively to the memos. In forming interest groups around the community organizations, as opposed to being assigned to a team or merely joining their friends on a team, students experience the following: (1) the student works with a community agency on a problem that he or she is really interested in exploring, and (2) students work in diverse groups that unite based on a common civic interest. In short, the students bond around issues, not personalities. These combinations enable students to collaborate with others whom they might not ordinarily work with, thus preparing them for diversity in the workplace.

The second document the teams produce is a *team-written proposal* to the organization in which they formally propose to do the documentation work. In this assignment, the students practice technical skills of document design and rhetorical skills of persuasion. Each student on the proposal writing team contributes a part of the proposal and the team then combines and edits the document as a whole online (see section on "Word Processor Collaboration Features"). The teams submit their proposal electronically and are required to get formal written feedback, also electronically, from the client about the status of their proposal; the students forward their acceptance via email to the instructor. The role of the instructor in all of these assignments is to stay in contact with the client periodically to validate the authenticity of what the students are doing and to "check in" with the client to make sure that everything is working satisfactorily and on schedule. The instructor guides the students in the work they are doing, explains and goes over the aspects of document production being practiced, and provides feedback to the students on their drafts.

The third document is the *service document* itself, which might be a brochure, PowerPoint presentation, questionnaire, set of instructions, report, poster or flyer, newsletter or any number of other professional documents. Again, the students work in teams to produce and edit the document (see "Using Blackboard" section). As the students work through this document, they send the fourth writing assignment to the client, which is a *progress report* on the state of production of the service document. As with all of the other documents in this *service-eLearning* project, the progress report is composed online and sent electronically. Both the justification memo and progress report can be written individually by each team member with the best one from each team chosen as the representative one to actually be sent to the client. All the work need not be teamwork. The final service document (the "deliverable") is also sent electronically so that the client can update data or tweak data and visuals as he or she sees fit. In essence, all of these linked assignments can be delivered, shared, created and edited online for a fully online *service-eLearning* experience.

The final writing task in this *service-eLearning* course model is the *reflection questionnaire*. Here students answer questions that assess citizenship and professional communication course competencies. Sample questions might include "How has your experience this semester made you think differently about your civic involvement?" or "What have you learned about working on a writing team?" According to scholars, reflection is key to learning: "we learn through combinations of thought and action, reflection and practice, theory and application" (Jacoby, 1996, pp. 6–7). Also, because service-learning projects focus student learning on larger social needs behind the writing that is being done, students need a venue for thinking about social issues and the part they are playing in doing something about community and social problems. By posting reflection questionnaires to Blackboard and allowing students to submit their responses privately to the instructor, the teacher allows students an environment in which they can be candid and open about their service experiences.

Using Blackboard to Create Documents and Collaborate Online

Online communication tools best augment service-learning by providing a platform for tracking, sharing and assessing. The Blackboard course management platform, for example, offers an assignment area, a grade book, and a document storage area. Thus, by posting assignment prompts for the justification memo, formal proposal, service document, and service-learning reflection questions, an instructor can deliver assignments to students in the order they would most likely encounter similar tasks in a workplace environment. Students would see the steps necessary to complete their project and learn about procedure. Blackboard functionality offers a way to collect and organize student work. After the submission deadline for the justification memo, for example, an instructor can collect each student's memo in one file. Students will both find and submit assignments through Blackboard. Here, as well as on discussion boards, students can submit their reflections on what they have learned about citizenship and professional communication throughout the *service-eLearning* project.

Electronic Mail. eLearning enhances actual learning in addition to creating an effective way to manage the learning process. First, students have the opportunity to work with their clients via email, as students may find it difficult (and not feasible in a fully online course) to set up face-to-face meetings with clients. Given the limits of a typical semester, including their class preparation and learning time, students must efficiently manage their time to effectively work with their clients. Second, email simplifies the communication process among students working in hybrid or fully-online collaborative groups, allowing them to negotiate each member's duties and set agendas via email rather than trying to determine when they can meet in person to manage their responsibilities. Third, communicating via email also gives instructors the opportunity to assess student progress, as students merely need to include their instructor's email address in the "cc" or "bcc" line when communicating with their clients. Instructors can see how their students are conducting their projects without waiting for the next class period, waiting for students to "check in" via email, or waiting for a scheduled conference.

As students are working on their projects, instructors can quickly offer advice and feedback via email. Since students primarily work on creating documents for clients, such communication enables students to more quickly revise their work and, most important, keep their clients abreast of project progress. By attaching drafts-in-progress of the document to the client, students can offer the client the opportunity to suggest revisions before the document is completed and before presentation of the deliverable.

Discussion Boards. Blackboard offers discussion boards as another venue through which all student teams can communicate with each other. At the least, a discussion board might include a thread in which students can introduce themselves to each other (and possibly clients, if given guest permissions) and ask questions. A more comprehensive discussion board might also include sections for each major assignment, with links to the assignment prompts.

The primary advantage of discussion boards is that if students post questions about their projects, students on other teams can offer help and the instructor can field questions that more than one team may encounter. In addition, students can use the discussion board to share work progress and reflect on their *service-eLearning* projects while instructors can use the discussion board to offer additional help for difficult writing or communication issues. Since students can attach files to discussion board posts, each team can offer online presentations of their *service-eLearning* project with attached graphics or handouts. Students can share their projects, how they managed their projects, and what they learned during their projects.

Group Pages. The optional Group Pages that Blackboard offers further enhances student work because each student team can set up its own group page as an online "home base." Blackboard's Group Pages offer a private electronic space where team members can access a file exchange feature, a discussion board, a chat room, and a team email server; additionally, the instructor can assign moderator privileges to the team leader, thus giving student team members control over the structure of their online meeting area. Since team members can store all of their drafts, revisions, and discussions in the Group Pages, instructors can easily assess the productivity of each student.

Rather than relying on email or f2f meetings, team members can use the Group Page discussion board to manage their own projects. The asynchronous format of discussion boards allows team members to easily see each other's contributions and allows team members to review previous discussions. Though team members can communicate solely via email, the discussion board saves team communication in one location and members' comments are not easily deleted or misfiled. In addition, since students can attach files to discussion board posts, they can discuss revisions of their *service-eLearning* project on the discussion board.

The File Exchange feature allows team members to send files to each other or to the whole team. Thus, two members working on part of the *service-eLearning* document could privately exchange revisions through the file exchange server or the team leader could send updated drafts of the document to team members via the file server. The file server can also serve as a backup file repository where team members can store drafts.

Word Processor Collaboration Features. Students can edit their documents using the collaboration features common to most word processors (e.g., Track Changes in Microsoft Word and Record Changes in Open Office). Some collaborators email documents to each other and then make editing comments in all caps, bold text or colored text; however, the collaboration feature in word processors eliminates the need to do this. For example, if the team leader were to send a draft of the *service-eLearning* document to each team member for revision, then the team members would simply need to enable the collaboration feature. The collaboration feature identifies changes and comments that each team member makes to the document by automatically coloring those comments and labeling them with the team member's name. If more than one team member edits the same document, each editor's comments will appear in a different color.

The collaboration feature in word processors helps team members work on projects through email. After separate team members make editing comments and revisions to a document, they can email or transfer the document to the team leader, who then can use the Merge feature available in most word processors to merge separate edits of the same document. The team leader then can send the merged document to the team members so they can review each other's revisions, suggestions and comments. Likewise, team members often will write different sections of their *service-eLearning* documents and then merge those sections to create their final document. After each member finishes final edits of his or her section, he or she can send it to the team leader to merge into the final *service-eLearning* document.

SERVICE-eLEARNING: STAKEHOLDER BENEFITS

Reflecting on our experience facilitating *service-eLearning* practice, we can say that although there were frequent technology glitches and occasional communication issues with community partners, the benefits to the students made the effort worthwhile. We have received positive feedback and appreciative comments from our community partners. An administrator from one organization had this to say about the brochure our students produced for her: "What an extraordinary job you all did! We are so excited about this! . . . Great job, teamwork, and commitment to making the project a success while overcoming the real world challenges that professionals face." She also wrote, "Overall we give you a big A+" (a comment much appreciated by the students). Students in our classes in general also reflected in positive ways. One student wrote on her reflection questionnaire, "I think I should help society out more. There is a lot to be done in the world and I know I can help."

As *service-eLearning* practitioners, we are gratified to see the positive impact of these methodologies on our students and community service organizations. Further study of other programs regionally or nationwide would be necessary to show broader impact of this pedagogy. While our experience is limited, nevertheless, our student and community partner feedback substantiates the research that supports both service-learning and online learning as valuable to students' education and development as citizens.

If college writing courses are to prepare all students (on-campus and online) for the kinds of writing that they will do in future, as well as prepare them for citizenship, it is important to think about incorporating *service-eLearning* into our professional writing courses. *Service-eLearning* has the potential to help develop students for the workplace in all its social and technological diversity.

NOTE

1. Ideas for constructing *service-eLearning* at Bemidji State University in Minnesota were presented by Jean Strait and Tim Sauer and published in *Educause Quarterly* (2004). Their ideas, however, included among other activities, a f2f component of the project, which will not work for fully online courses. The authors acknowledge their ideas as the "birth of e-service."

CHAPTER 8

SERVICE-eLEARNING

Meeting the Objectives of Community-Based Nursing Education

Christopher W. Blackwell

Community-based nursing education (CBNE) programs have emerged across the United States over the past decade, shifting the clinical education of nurses from a traditional inpatient setting to outpatient, ambulatory, and community-centered treatment facilities (Ervin, Bickes, & Myers Schim, 2006). Beyond care provided to diverse client bases, CBNE also provides an opportunity for nursing students to experience service-learning as they meet course objectives within the community. According to Laurie DiPadova-Stocks, (2005), service-learning is "[a]n academically rigorous instructional method that incorporates meaningful community service into the curriculum. Focusing on critical, reflective thinking and civic responsibility, service-learning involves students in organized community service that addresses local needs, while developing their academic skills, respect for others, and commitment to the common good" (p. 345). A *service-eLearning* approach enhances students' ability to meet course objectives while also promoting achievement of course and service-learning out-

Service-eLearning: Educating for Citizenship, pages 87–94
Copyright © 2008 by Information Age Publishing
All rights of reproduction in any form reserved.

comes. This chapter examines the role of a hybrid, Web-mediated physical and mental health course within a CBNE curriculum and explores how online components of the course enhanced student learning outcomes.

SERVICE-LEARNING IN COMMUNITY-BASED NURSING EDUCATION (CBNE)

CBNE programs concentrate clinical nursing education experiences in community and public health settings and focus on primary and secondary prevention and treatment strategies (American Association of Colleges of Nursing, 2002). The CBNE curriculum was created as a result of data emerging in the early 1990s that suggested advances in healthcare, cost containment, health financing, and reimbursement shifts were driving patient care from inpatient to outpatient ambulatory and community-based settings (Ervin et al., 2006). In 2002, the American Association of Colleges of Nursing (AACN) authored a guide entitled "Moving Forward with Community-Based Nursing Education" to help ease the transition from a traditional hospital-based nursing education curriculum to a community-based nursing education program.

These programs enrich the learning experience of nurses by fulfilling many of the objectives of service-learning. DiPadova-Stocks (2005) identified objectives of service-learning. These include: (1) placing students in organized community service that addresses local needs; (2) developing academic skills, and (3) fostering respect for others. The following discussion assesses the role of a *service-eLearning* physical and mental health course in a community-based nursing education program in meeting these three objectives. Strong partnerships among academia, community agencies, and service providers are needed to meet healthcare needs of underserved populations (Beauchesne & Meservey, 1999). This trinity serves as the infrastructure of CBNE and is also a distinctive characteristic of service-learning.

Many researchers have supported a strong service-learning connection with nursing education. The National Service-Learning Clearinghouse (2004) published a bibliography of works examining the role of service-learning in nursing education. As of this writing, the database contained 55 published writings on the subject. More work is needed to explore the benefits of service-learning in CBNE, in particular the ways that eLearning can enhance these pedagogies.

SERVICE-eLEARNING IN A HYBRID CBNE COURSE

In the undergraduate nursing program at the University of Central Florida, the required course "Promoting Physical and Mental Health in the Community" is a hybrid course wherein some of the in-person classroom meetings are substituted for participation in online learning activities. The course is a total of nine credit hours, five of which are classroom-based and four of which are clinical-based. Classroom instruction is enhanced with an extensive online component. Students access the eLearning, Web-based portions of the course through the University's online teaching interface (WebCT) and are able to download the course syllabus, assignments, and laboratory outlines. Clinically, students complete rotations in community and public health nursing, community mental health nursing, and long-term care and submit selected assignments via the WebCT interface.

Examples of community and public health nursing experiences include working in screening and primary care clinics in public schools and health departments and administering immunizations to pediatric and special-needs populations within the community. Community mental health experiences might include such activities as working in psychiatric crisis units within a county health department; assisting addicted clients in short-term residential treatment facilities; and providing mental health assessments for high-risk student populations within the public school system.

Long-term care clinical settings include both nursing homes and skilled nursing facilities. During these clinical experiences, students work with short- and long-term residential clients in both private and public facilities and nursing homes. While the timing of the placement of students within these clinical rotations varies throughout the academic semester, all rotations have online interaction requirements designed to reinforce the concepts being taught. Students electronically submit weekly journals in which they demonstrate personal insight into their clinical experiences and progress in meeting course objectives.

Students also use the WebCT discussion boards to discuss specific client encounters and issues with their peers, to critically analyze instructor-posted case studies, and to provide evidence-based nursing interventions and rationales for client care. Each clinical instructor for the course has full access to the online components through WebCT and uses the online components to maximize communication with students through group discussion and email. Utilizing *service-eLearning* in a hybrid physical and mental health course met the three primary aims of service-learning, while also addressing the complementary goals of CBNE.

Placing Students in Organized Community Service that Addresses Local Needs

Community-based nursing centers (CNCs) are an integral component of many community-based nursing education programs (Wink, 2001). CNCs serve to educate nursing students in community settings while also providing outreach efforts to often underserved client populations. These clinical settings are not necessarily nurse-managed clinics (Wink, 2001) but instead are directed activities within a given community that are based from a centralized location (such as a senior citizen center or a school). CNCs have a strong primary care and preventative focus (Tagliareni & King, 2006). A recent study assessing the makeup of clients served through CNCs found that: "Although the location for the health promotion and disease-prevention activities varied, 21% of group activities occurred in schools, ranging from preschools and head start programs (9%) to elementary (6%), middle (4%), and high school (2%), and 26% were conducted in a nursing center or senior citizens' facility, with the remaining 50% conducted in various community locations, including public housing facilities. In contrast, only 5% of individual encounters occurred in school settings, with the majority conducted in the nursing wellness centers or in senior citizens' housing facilities" (Tagliareni & King, 2006, p. 25).This research also highlighted the impact CNCs have on minority populations, many of which suffer from a variety of health disparities. M. Elaine Tagliareni & Eunice S. King (2006) found considerable variation in their analysis of clients served in the CNCs they sampled: "Slightly more than half of the participants in the group programs were of African American ethnicity (54%), followed by white (24%), Asian (3%), and other (19%). Among the individual encounters assessed by the researchers, almost half (49%) were with white clients, followed by African American (26%), Asian (5%), and other races or combinations (20%)" (Tagliareni & King, 2006, pp. 20–26). These statistics solidify the role CNCs have in meeting the needs of a particular local community as well as fostering respect for others through student exposure to cultures that may be different from their own. Both of these outcomes are identified objectives of service-learning (DiPadova-Stocks, 2005).

Two of the objectives for the hybrid physical and mental health course are: (1) To provide holistic nursing care for clients of all ages with physical and mental health problems in rehabilitation, long term care and mental health settings based on a biopsychosocial approach; and (2) to practice delivery of care to groups, utilizing concepts of group dynamics and educational principles.

An eLearning-based evaluation method employed by clinical instructors to ensure students are completing these objectives is the completion of a weekly journal. Students submit an online journal for their clinical instructor to review, which assesses whether or not students are meeting the objectives of the course, identifies which objectives are not being met, and also establishes a plan of how the student will meet the objective in future clinical experiences. Beyond online clinical journals which students are required to complete weekly, students also participate in discussion board postings regarding their clinical experiences for the week.

Students identify and discuss some of the implications for nursing care they learned from their clinical experience during the week. Because students are often separated and placed in various clinical sites throughout the community, they benefit from reading the online discussion boards regarding the clinical knowledge and advice gained by their cohorts who might have been providing services to an entirely different group of clients in an entirely different clinical setting.

CBNE and clinical exposure to diverse populations afford student nurses the opportunity to address needs of local residents within a particular community. Online networking with peers also advances the students' perceptions and comprehension of health disparities among specific minority groups within a particular community. Lynn Clark Callister and Debra Hobbins-Garbett (2000) supported this in their study which assessed how nursing students achieve service-learning objectives. Students assessed by the researchers indicated that one of the strongest benefits of service-learning was an increased awareness of unmet needs in clients, families, communities, and populations.

Developing Academic Skills

CBNE programs extrapolate the skills necessary for appropriate health assessment of pediatric, adult, and geriatric clients while also extending assessment skills into the community setting. Nursing students enrolled in the "Promoting Physical and Mental Health" Hybrid course discussed in this chapter complete a family case study, which emphasizes assessment techniques for a family living within a particular community. The case study is downloaded from the WebCT platform and students are able to download the document and manipulate their input via a word processing program. Making the document electronically accessible from the course's WebCT component allows students to augment their computing skills by increasing their exposure to computer-based data retrieval.

Jane Eshlemann and Ruth Davidhizar (2000) highlighted the significance of community assessment projects in developing nursing students' overall assessment skills. The experiences gained from these types of assessment projects enable students to use the nursing process in a basic community assessment as well as provide community decision makers and stakeholders with significant data and analyses about the health-related needs and potential solutions within a particular community (Eshlemann & Davidhizar, 2000). The eLearning portions of the course can also serve as a means of communication between students and also provide an enhancement in their understanding of community assessment principles and concepts. Students are able to post their final completed assessment study on the WebCT discussion boards; all members of the class have access to these discussion boards and each student's case study is available for every member of the course to review.

eLearning course components help to solidify the gap between didactic learning and clinical learning. Lee-Anne Gassner and Karen Wooten (1999) found that experiential learning was greatly enhanced through stronger collaboration between students, clinicians, and nursing faculty. Hybrid courses help to increase this collaboration largely through an increased influx of communication between students, clinicians, and faculty. Interactions and feedback are faster and implemented in a more academic fashion. In addition, instructors are able to teach concepts to a greater number of students by increasing the potential for interaction and the use of group discussions to illustrate course concepts.

Fostering Respect for Others

An important concept student nurses must understand during the course of their education is the concept of autonomy (Potter & Perry, 2005). One aspect of autonomy is gaining insight and respect for individual client decision making. For example, a client in the end-stages of cancer may choose to discontinue caustic chemotherapeutic regimens despite the possibility of prolonging life for a few more months. The nurse may feel disappointment in the client's decision, but ultimately, he or she must respect the decisions rendered by the client.

It is essential that nurses be prepared and educated on how to communicate with clients in the end-stages of life before they actually have real interactions with such clients. One approach to introduce students to the concepts of death and dying is through case studies. Students learn through simulation the appropriate techniques involved in effectively and therapeutically communicating with dying clients and their loved ones. The physical and mental health course discussed in this chapter includes extensive laboratory and simulation training through the course's skills lab component.

One section of the course's lab specifically addresses death and dying. Students are placed in preselected groups and presented with several plausible clinical scenarios and lead through the nursing process with the assistance of a laboratory instructor. A designated student leader or leaders assist in the laboratory discussions. All of the scenarios are downloaded from the course in WebCT. Students also have their own discussion board sections and collaborate collectively prior to the laboratory session electronically. Analysis of student performance is achieved through evaluation from not only the instructor but fellow students within the group as well.

Through simulated learning, students are better prepared to act when they encounter similar clinical situations in their actual clinical courses. In CBNE, students may be treating a dying client through a hospice setting, providing holistic and palliative nursing care to clients who have little life expectancy. After participating in online group discussions and simulated laboratory exercises, students are not totally new to these clients' needs and at least have a small knowledge base regarding the most effective approach to treating these clients. Students gain the skills necessary to respect the client's decisions and through the eLearning component of the course, reinforce the concepts of autonomy in service delivery.

STUDENT, FACULTY, AND COMMUNITY PARTNER RESPONSES

Qualitative responses students provided on formal evaluations of the course highlight the impact these laboratory preparation sessions have in providing client care. For example, students expressed greater understanding and comprehension of therapeutic communication principles related to death and dying. In addition, feedback indicated that many students appreciate the easy access the eLearning component provides to documents and case studies that assist them in preparing for their simulation laboratory experiences. Because the online environment provides a virtual meeting room, students in varying geographic locations are able to interact via the course's discussion boards, affording greater opportunity for collaboration.

Students also use the eLearning components of the hybrid course to reinforce and reflect on the concepts taught in the simulation labs. For example, students might discuss in later online journal entries or online discussions about their personal clinical experiences and how the simulation labs provided a greater understanding of the clinical concepts. Several students have commented to instructors that the eLearning component of the course afforded easier communication with faculty and fellow students. For example, one comment written by an anonymous student in a course evaluation stated: "I like how we can use the WebCT discussion boards to talk about clinical situations and plan group projects. Many of us live miles away from each other and the WebCT boards sure make planning easier! Plus, it's great for sharing thoughts and ideas about clinical experiences and providing useful clinical information to each other."

In turn, faculty also expressed this positive aspect of the course's Web component. One clinical instructor stated: "Using the course's WebCT Site allows me to have easy access to communication with the students and gives me the opportunity to quickly share student experiences with others. This allows me to reinforce clinical concepts students encounter, such as the importance of the nurse respecting clients' personal decisions about their health care, to other members of the clinical group. It also gives students the opportunity to interact by posting their personal reflections and experiences on these concepts" (S. Ladores, personal communication, February 21, 2007).

Finally, clinical partners within the community can also be granted access to the WebCT Sites for communication with students. Although this is not currently utilized, user identification numbers and security passwords can be registered to individuals in the community who need access to the course's WebCT Site. This allows these individuals the opportunity to communicate with students and enhance their online learning experience.

COURSE REFLECTION

A hybrid, *service-eLearning* approach to physical and mental health curriculum plays a crucial role in meeting the objectives of service-learning and CBNE. Through various integrations of online enhancements in service-learning approaches, students placed in organized community services more effectively address local needs, develop academic skills, and foster respect for others. eLearning provides an invaluable contribution to nursing students' abilities to provide nursing care in community-based settings. Although the context of this discussion has focused on nursing education and more specifically, CBNE, the application of these concepts extrapolates into any discipline that utilizes eLearning to facilitate a service-learning approach to instruction. These approaches to service-learning lend to the enhancement of communication, collaboration, group discussion, and overall facilitation of learning for students engaged in this highly rewarding and significant form of learning. Through continuous innovation of the uses of eLearning strategies, every academic discipline can strengthen how their unique students meet their own objectives of service-learning.

CHAPTER 9

CREATING INTERNATIONAL, MULTIDISCIPLINARY, SERVICE-eLEARNING EXPERIENCES

**Hilary E. Kahn, Sarah M. Stelzner, Mary E. Riner,
Armando E. Soto-Rojas, Joan Henkle,
M. Humberto A. Veras Godoy, José L. Antón de la Concha,
and E. Angeles Martínez-Mier**

Increasing the cultural and linguistic effectiveness of health providers and their understanding of the pervasiveness of culture itself can reduce barriers to effective care. International service-learning experiences allow health professions students the opportunity to work in communities where patients have emigrated from, contributing to a deeper and more applied understanding of cultural differences. However, faculty in any cultural immersion or study abroad program face challenges to develop and facilitate these experiences. Online technologies can be used to decrease these challenges and enhance learning. This chapter describes an international service-learning course that incorporated eLearning to facilitate communication, cultural adaptation, and learning outcomes.

Service-eLearning: Educating for Citizenship, pages 95–105

Health professions' students and faculty from Mexico and the United States participated in Web-based videoconferences to plan collaborative work, engage in team-building activities, conduct assessments and teach joint classes. Students participated in a videoconference that allowed them to learn about each other's culture by discussing the cultural and personal significance of photographs. Ninety-five percent of students agreed that these sessions were relevant to the program, and faculty evaluations reported significant advantages with the use of online technology. Therefore, our experiences suggest that online technologies enhance learning outcomes and increase communication and understanding of culture and cultural differences in international service-learning environments.

THE CHALLENGE OF PREPARING LEARNERS FOR GLOBAL CIVIC ENGAGEMENT

In spite of the continuous contact that health professions students have with Spanish-speaking patients, most have little understanding of the pervasiveness and complexity of their culture or beliefs. This absence of understanding may be a barrier to culturally appropriate and cost effective medical and dental care. In fact, several studies on access barriers to health care for Latino children have identified cultural and language differences as one of the major access barriers to health care (Carter-Pokras, O'Neill & Soleras 2004; Flores et al., 1998; Flores & Vega, 1998).

Ultimately, it is health professions training programs that must provide a variety of experiences to improve training of health care providers to serve an increasingly diverse community. International service-learning programs in Latin America can provide these educational contexts by allowing students to work directly in the communities from where Latino patients emigrate. As a result, students develop a greater appreciation of the role of culture, cultural differences, and various definitions of illness, health and healing, which are critical in providing quality health care. Research studies have linked international immersion experiences with enhanced development of both language and cultural sensitivity skills (Bissonette & Route, 1994; Godkin & Savagiau, 2001).

The service-learning model, which provides a deeper level of student engagement, is ideally suited to improve patient–provider communication and to increase cultural awareness. As an active learning strategy, service-learning contributes to the development of health professions competencies in a variety of domains. Studies have reported that service-learning facilitates cross-cultural understanding, reduces stereotypes and increases one's ability to solve complex problems in real settings (Boyle-Baise, 1998; Rust et al., 2006). Students learn by acquiring, applying, and reflecting on the skills, knowledge, and awareness that are components of intercultural competency (Ashwill, 2004). International service-learning augments the learning outcomes and creates a framework that provides the principles of excellence as outlined by the American Association of Colleges & Universities' National Leadership Council Report, *College Learning for the New Global Century* (2006). This report reveals how immersion, problem solving, the harnessing of technologies, engagement of global questions and real-world problems, and knowledge and skills of cultural literacy, global knowledge, civic engagement, and project-based learning are essential learning outcomes for every institution of higher education in the 21st century. International service-learning becomes a microcosm of this educational framework and it is this ability to draw upon all of the essential outcomes that make it such a powerful pedagogy.

However, the collaborations needed to develop successful international service-learning experiences face unique challenges. Among those, the barriers most difficult to overcome include cost, time and loss of meaning without the face to face component. Despite their difficulties, international academic collaborations pose many advantages which make them worth pursuing. Such collaborations provide health professions students with exposure to diverse options for future professional career development by observing first-hand the collaborative work between both practicing professionals and researchers. Participating students also gain perspective on differences of health care system across countries.

The use of online learning technologies may aid in eliminating some of the barriers faced by international collaborations that include a service-learning component by enlivening the curricula and broadening the scope of service-learning initiatives. It has been suggested that online technologies, when appropriately employed, may enhance student learning outcomes and increase communication and understanding in distance learning settings (Gobbo et al., 2004). Online technology can break down the cultural, political, and geographic barriers that prevent fluid collaboration, providing environments for social interaction and bi-national academic endeavors. Virtual classrooms facilitate equitable access and create forums for reflection, cross-cultural navigation, and for a variety of learning styles (Gobbo et al., 2004).

INTERNATIONAL, MULTIDISCIPLINARY COLLABORATIONS

Description of Service-eLearning Partnership

The international, multidisciplinary *service-eLearning* project at Indiana University Purdue University at Indianapolis (IUPUI) began eight years ago. As part of a semester long service-learning course, health professions' students and faculty live and work for seven to eight days in a small rural community, Calnali, in the State of Hidalgo, Mexico. The participants include multidisciplinary, bi-national dental, medical, nursing, public health and social work students and faculty advisors from IUPUI and Universidad Autonoma del Estado de Hidalgo (UAEH). Support from non-academic units such as the "Center for Service and Learning" and the "Office of International Affairs" at IUPUI have enhanced the components of cultural orientation, service-learning and international education. A partnership with local health workers in Mexico and with public health officials from Hidalgo has been established and a formal written agreement with the local authorities in Calnali and UAEH has been signed. Thus, the true partnership involves IUPUI and UAEH health professions students and faculty, the community of Calnali, Friends of Hidalgo, a small nonprofit organization that supports multiple capacity building efforts in the town and state, and public health officials in Hidalgo. The interactive video meetings facilitated communication and engagement between various parties: including university authorities (administrators and faculty), health state and/or municipal authorities and faculty/students, and communication between students.

Description of eLearning Activities.   The necessary equipment and infrastructure for videoconferencing continue to become more accessible, reliable, and affordable, particularly with the utilization of an IP (Internet Protocol) connection, accessible for no charge through the Internet. At IUPUI, the videoconference system is a Polycom VSX 7000, which operates via IP and utilizes the H323 standard. Other supporting equipment include a projector, a screen or TV monitor, sound system, and microphone.

Preparation sessions for the Mexico service-learning experience are part of a formal multidisciplinary graduate-level course, which is developed and supported by a two-year educational grant. As a prerequisite for participating in the project, multidisciplinary students attend sessions that include the following topics: the history of immigration from Mexico; the immigrant perspective; traditional health beliefs and changing focus from individual patients to communities of patients and common health problems in Mexico and in immigrants to Indiana. Videoconference sessions on these topics and others were scheduled to facilitate engagement between students and faculty from IUPUI and the UAEH.

Goals of the videoconferences for students and faculty who participate in the service-learning program were to: (a) engage in team-building through participating in cultural engagement activities, developing a work plan for the week service-learning experiences, and engaging in personal reflective questions that will promote deep awareness of the benefits of involvement in the outreach program, (b) develop a practical and cultural understanding of the health professions education and health care delivery systems in both the state of Hidalgo and Indiana through joint presentations by faculty and students in the medical, dental, and nursing schools of each university; (c) plan for collaborative work arrangements for both group education sessions and clinic primary care services, and (d) assess the total experience: including pre-trip preparation, onsite activities, post-trip personal reflection and group evaluation with recommendations for future trips.

Faculty from IUPUI, UAEH and staff from the Hidalgo State Health Department utilize videoconference technology to jointly teach a session to explore Hidalgo's state and local health profiles. The most common medical and dental problems observed in Calnali are reviewed based on a joint IUPUI/UAEH study of previous years' diagnoses. Additionally, in 2006, faculty designed an assignment where photographs were used as educational tools in an effort to facilitate team-building activities and deepen cultural understanding. This interactive instructional technique allowed students to engage with one another and learn about culture through a dynamic interactive component; it was designed to initiate dialogue and facilitate discussion on cultural differences and similarities. The assignment was created based on the assumption that photographs document and record successes and life passages. Students were asked to select a home photograph that had themselves represented in a social context (such as eating at home, playing at a park, vacationing, attending a concert, going to school, relaxing with friends, etc.). Students were informed that the photograph would be used to initiate discussion on cultural diversity, and they were guided to consider choosing an image that had some cultural or personal significance. Students were asked to share this image not only with their individual partner but with the entire group from IUPUI and UAEH, and to discuss its personal, cultural, and family meaning.

Faculty members from UAEH and IUPUI organized all the photos into an electronic presentation that was sent to the partner institution and sent to assigned student partners via email. In preparation for the videoconference, students looked at the photos sent to them from the partner institution and considered their cultural, personal, social, and family significance prior to the group videoconference.

Partnered students at IUPUI and UAEH wrote short paragraphs (in Spanish and/or English) about the cultural and personal significance of the image from their partner abroad. Students were asked to (a) interpret the cultural significance of the photo, (b) consider the personal meaning to the individual and/or family and (c) consider what the photograph said about family in that culture. Students were also asked questions about the social context of the photograph, (for example, who took the picture, who posed the people, and where had the photograph been displayed prior to this assignment?). The latter questions allowed the group to get beyond the final product of family photographs and into the cultural processes behind them (Chalfen, 1992). Although many of the IUPUI students and faculty were bilingual, fewer UAEH faculty and students shared this proficiency; hence, students were allowed to write the essay in their preferred language and during the videoconference, while bilingual faculty from both institutions interpreted the discussion and translated the written presentations.

Photograph owners were not allowed to participate in these initial cultural discussions, but were later expected to inform the class about information their peers assumed correctly or incorrectly regarding their photographs. Class discussion followed each owner's commentary. Faculty members and students worked to unearth reasons why any errors in the interpretation of the photograph may have occurred. The group discussed how cultural, gender, religious, racial, age, socioeconomic, or ethnic differences may have played a role in the misreading of the photograph.

The interactive and integrated pedagogy had multiple functions. It was an "ice-breaking" activity to initiate dialogue with students from the partner institution. The methodology provided an interactive forum for students to learn about cultural content of the photographs and for students to reveal their cultural values and beliefs. It promoted critical analysis and observational skills. Lastly, the methodology revealed the pervasiveness and complexity of culture, which is a vital outcome of developing cultural competency. To become culturally competent, students should not only understand and be able to navigate cultural differences, but they should also intimately know how culture influences every action, thought, idea, professional practice, and even the way a photograph is constructed and given meaning. In short, it was a structured cultural experience.

Post-Experience Videoconference. Approximately two months after the completion of the experience, faculty and student service-learning assistants from IUPUI and faculty from UAEH held an online videoconference to: (1) formally present findings of the evaluation from IUPUI students, (2) discuss funding opportunities in both the US and Mexico, and (3) plan for 2006–2007 collaborative work as Strategic Partner efforts on the IUPUI campus. The roles of student service-learning assistants to organize the student experience, finish data collection, develop a retreat for Calnali organizers and plan the structured orientation for future international service-learning experiences in Mexico were also discussed.

Exploration of State and Local Health Profiles via Videoconference. An additional videoconference was conducted to learn more about the health status of Hidalgo residents and to share research findings from a study conducted the previous year. Following introductions, the assistant director of the Hidalgo state health department provided an epidemiologic overview of the primary health concerns for people within the state. This overview provided a health profile of the residents that would be receiving services in Calnali, in addition to a question/answer session.

The videoconference continued with preliminary research findings from a study collaboratively conducted by the two universities the previous year. The presenters consisted of the research team members, including graduate and undergraduate students and faculty. A PowerPoint presentation had been developed and was displayed during the conference with the information on each slide in English and Spanish. Using a standard research presentation format allowed the opportunity for students to create their professional research presentation to peers and faculty.

Students who had participated in the program the previous year were made aware of the study conducted and grew eager to learn of the outcomes, particularly in the ways they helped shape the services provided in the upcoming service trip. An action-research study was conducted to gain resident perceptions of their major health problems, potential causes and possible solution. The preliminary findings revealed that residents were interested in gaining more information about their health problems and potential causes, identifying the need to further integrate patient education into the clinical services. Such realization led the team to integrate a new health education station to provide information about a variety of health topics including self-breast examination for women, prevention of cancer through not using tobacco, and increasing food preparation hygiene.

Assessment Tools. A formal assessment questionnaire was developed and distributed to IUPUI students to evaluate the *service-eLearning* experience using videoconference technology. In addition to posing open-ended questions to solicit student comments, the evaluation questionnaire gathered information about the educational sessions and photograph assignment using a five-point Likert-scale. Upon conclusion of the last videoconference, an IUPUI faculty retreat was organized to provide an opportunity to review the program history, assess objectives, and reflect on past successes and challenges. The retreat also allowed opportunity to plan for the immediate future and work with those directly involved in the program toward developing a strategic plan in anticipation for the next 5–10 years, focusing on the balance between academic and community interests.

STUDENT ASSESSMENT OF THE
SERVICE-eLEARNING EXPERIENCE

Assessing this experience reinforced the value of online learning technologies into service-learning experiences to create a *service-eLearning* approach (See Table 9.1). Ninety-five percent of the students agreed or strongly agreed that attending the preparatory sessions were helpful and relevant to the project. Working with Mexican health professionals was mentioned as a definite advantage by several of the students. Of the twenty-four IUPUI

TABLE 9.1   Student Evaluations of Relevance and Usefulness to Project

	Percentage		
Information	Agreed or strongly agreed	Neither agreed nor disagreed	Disagreed or strongly disagreed
Attending preparatory sessions	95	2.5	2.5
Participation in photographic sessions	78	12	10
Participation in videoconference on common health issues in Hidalgo	67	18	15

students and twenty-six UAEH students participating in the photographs assignment, seventy-eight percent strongly agreed/agreed that the photograph activity was relevant to their activities in Calnali. Sixty-seven percent of students agreed the videoconference presentation of common health issues in Hidalgo (presented by the Commission of Public Health in Hidalgo with UAEH and the Family Health Needs study) was helpful and relevant to the project. Students identified (1) team work, (2) collaboration with UAEH, and (3) integration with UAEH students, among the program strengths. Those identified strengths were specifically enhanced by eLearning because the technology facilitated deeper levels of engagement, communication, and collaboration. *Service-eLearning* enabled an active dimension of integrated education that fostered team work and promoted cross-cultural communication.

Furthermore, (1) team work, (2) collaboration with UAEH, and (3) the interdisciplinary approach and integration with UAEH, were ranked among the top three program strengths by the faculty attending the retreat. Again, the use of eLearning was an integral part of faculty teamwork building and interdisciplinary activities. It specifically engaged UAEH and public health officials regarding topics they need to have us prepare and that they would be comfortable giving to our group. For example, as a result of the videoconferencing with UAEH faculty and students, communication between a new public health faculty member and two UAEH faculty members about an upcoming study was facilitated. Such increased communication fostered by videoconferencing facilitated a positive outcome for faculty.

Multidisciplinary faculty members have expressed benefits of participation in the program. They reported a deeper knowledge of: (1) how much students appreciated the learning and serving alongside students from other disciplines enabled by the eLearning technology; (2) a greater understanding of how to develop effective communication among the faculty program directors. Specific excerpts from anonymous student comments and suggestions to improve the videoconference activities included the following:

> ... The ability to learn and work with students from a different culture is the one of the major strengths of this program"; "... The strengths of the program are multiple: great team work, great services provided, everyone did a super job and the experience is truly life changing"; "... I thought all of the talks this year were relevant and interesting. In the future students might benefit from a session detailing how the health system really works in Mexico"; "I think the first (videoconference) session should be used to go over the basics of the trip—who's going, what we're going to be doing, logistics, who we're partnering with and why."

Student comments demonstrated the benefits of eLearning. Cross-cultural engagement, deeper learning, and skills of collaboration were resulting outcomes from the use of interactive technology. Student suggestions for improvement built on the existing strengths and capacities of the technology and confirmed the value of a *service-eLearning* approach to international, multicultural education.

BENEFITS AND RECOMMENDATIONS FOR INTERNATIONAL, MULTIDISCIPLINARY SERVICE-eLEARNING

While reflecting upon the many facets of this project, it was evident that utilizing online videoconferencing enhanced the framework of international service-learning methodology. The online tools provided useful learning and relationship-building strategies for international experiences, accepted by multidisciplinary bi-national health professions students and faculty teams. Beginning to build the relationships prior to onsite work proved to be valuable in establishing effective collaborative work teams when students and faculty from both universities arrived in the community to provide health and education services. Furthermore, by using a blended team-building and health knowledge approach to the online technology sessions, the bi-national team was more aware of their teammates' cultural perspectives. Finally, sharing results of research collaborations increased team members' understanding of the benefits involved in conducting bi-national community based participatory research. This exposure can pave the way for the health professions' students to participate in bi-national, cross-cultural experiences in their future careers and better understand the breadth of cultural meanings.

The use of eLearning technology clearly alleviated some of the challenges faced by this service-learning program. The barriers to communication of cost, time and loss of meaning by not being face-to-face were partially eliminated by the use of online tools. This technology-mediated communication has enlivened the curricula and broadened the scope of the experience, particularly because the exploration of culture was led by students through interaction rather than lecture.

Our experiences support the recommendations made by Linda Drake Gobbo, Richard Rodman, Michael Nieckoski and Kirsten Sheppard (2004) who found that eLearning technologies, when appropriately employed, enhance student learning outcomes and increase communication and understanding in distance learning settings. The online learning technologies utilized in this program enabled deeper, more engaged student learning that not only provided professional skills, knowledge, and practice, but also broadened student understanding of international relations, global processes, and cultural complexity. The pre-departure orientation and international exchange were particularly important and useful for the hastening of cultural adaptation during what was, by all definitions, a brief service program abroad. In these cases, proper and thorough orientation and cultural sensitivity had to be instilled prior to arrival, since the health professions' students did not have extended time for traditional adaptation or in-country orientation. They were expected to be ready and prepared to practice their skills and apply their knowledge, and online technology aided their ability to be professionally and culturally-oriented upon arrival.

The impact of the use of eLearning and technology on the project was clearly documented by participant evaluations. Preparation sessions on common medical and dental problems were supported by the largest number of students and appeared to have the most positive or informative impact. These results supported the ability of this international *service-eLearning* to increase the awareness of binational health issues and health disparities in those students who participated through the use of Web-based videoconferencing in comprehensive and structured orientation and reflection. IUPUI students learned from Hidalgo state-level public health professionals about the health problems of the people they were going to be serving. This provided perspective on how the official public health presence is a universal aspect of the health care system across countries. In addition, inclusion of the research presentation demonstrated successful binational research collaboration. This type of collaboration between both practicing professionals and researchers provided health professions students from UAEH and IUPUI a paradigm for future professional career development that is specific in applicability yet global in scope.

Further, the videoconferencing format is clearly applicable to other programs, campuses, and disciplines. International service-learning programs and more traditional study abroad programs can certainly benefit from this type of interactive engagement for orientation, content delivery, and international dialogue. Working in multidisciplinary teams is also a unique methodology that strengthens student learning outcomes. In fact, a review of the competencies for students in schools of nursing, medicine and dentistry revealed that communication and the ability to work in multidisciplinary teams are key to graduation and success in the field. Clearly, these collaboration skills are role-modeled, tested and considered strengths of the program. Likewise, team work, the collaboration with UAEH, the interdisciplinary approach and the integration with UAEH, were ranked among the top three strengths of the program by the faculty. It is important that faculty engaging in similar interactive *service-eLearning* experiences clearly understand these competencies and define them, for themselves and their students, as learning goals and objectives.

Lessons were also learned about utilizing interactive video technology. One lesson learned was the necessity to schedule trial runs of the videoconferences with a smaller number of faculty and students to assure that the technology, connection, and timing are adequate to accommodate the binational and bilingual teaching format proposed. Faculty should receive basic training in the protocol in using such technology (in fact, partnering with technology experts and units is very important) and they must prepare their students for the activity by explaining the assignment, providing communication tips for videoconferencing, and defining the expected learning outcomes. Of course, students and faculty should also expect greater involvement in a lengthy orientation session, as it takes additional time for students to feel comfortable with the equipment, and the need to interpret discussions also lengthens the discussion time.

Conducting research collaboratively and through videoconference exchanges increased team members' understanding of research issues involved in the practice of binational exchanges. It enabled student-led learning and problem-solving in response to professional challenges, health concerns, and cultural situations. This first-hand cultural and practical exposure provided an international education and an immersion into professional health practices in a diverse cultural context. Overall, *Service-eLearning* allows health professions students to practice and successfully navigate binational and cross-cultural settings, whether in the United States or abroad and whether as health professionals or more broadly as globally-aware citizens.

PART III

MOVING FORWARD WITH
SERVICE-eLEARNING

CHAPTER 10

SHAPING THE UNSCRIPTED FUTURE

The Role of Service-eLearning

Laurie N. DiPadova-Stocks and Amber Dailey-Hebert

The United States is now sprinting out of the Industrial/Manufacturing Age through the Information/Knowledge-based/Technological global age—and beyond (Reich, 1992; Rifkin, 1996). Unprecedented changes affecting every aspect of life are occurring throughout the world. Perhaps the best-known work regarding the impacts on the United States, its workforce and global competitiveness, is Thomas Friedman's *The World is Flat* (2006) in which he details the economically flattening world and sets out possibilities for educators and students alike to address a massive set of interrelated changes. *Service-eLearning*, an integrative pedagogy and critical learning model, presents itself as an ideal pedagogy for the Unscripted Future we face—a future conceptualized broadly as the myriad of consequences (known and unknown) of the increasingly fast-paced, dynamic, and unpredictable changes in the global/economic/technological context of human life (DiPadova-Stocks, 2008).

Service-eLearning: Educating for Citizenship, pages 109–118
Copyright © 2008 by Information Age Publishing
All rights of reproduction in any form reserved.

FUTURES: SCRIPTED AND UNSCRIPTED

Obviously, in the existential sense, the future of each of us as individuals carries no guarantees. Each of us has an uncertain future. However, while life's inherent uncertainties cannot be erased, for many individuals the future has been somewhat predictable or scripted.

It is a long-held axiom of the social sciences that society provides a web of expectations that show the path for a predictable life in that society. Such expectations may be grounded initially in traditions and common beliefs, and in what sociologists term as norms and mores. In these societies the lives of children, as they grow into adults, tend to follow the same path as their parents—following a societal script.

As societies become more complex and pluralistic, and the norms and mores are found to differ between religious and ethnic groups and among socioeconomic classes, expectations of acceptable behavior become institutionalized in the workplace and even codified into law. The lives of parents still provide prospects regarding what the future holds for their children, but in many modern societies, opportunities to achieve beyond one's parents are prized.

In what can be termed the American script, the United States is known as the land of opportunity, a place where each generation has the potential to do better than the previous generation. This American script has been a beacon to the world, beckoning people to these shores for centuries. While unevenly applied due to aspects of inequality, in general with the American script, children learn to study hard in school, gain an education, progress in college in order to obtain a solid job with retirement and health insurance benefits, and also to secure a home mortgage—the largest investment most families make (Florida, 2005; Warren & Tvagi, 2003).

Education has played an indispensable role in the American script. By preparing people for society and the economy as we have known it, education has provided the key to opportunity that advances beyond one's parents. The GI Bill helped fund the education of thousands of veterans, one factor propelling the post-WWII era's dramatic growth of the middle class in the United States, spurring breathtaking advances in the sciences and technology. The academic disciplines provide the frameworks and the content-specific knowledge that permit people to navigate successfully among society's sectors, institutions, and organizations. Thus, with educational advancement and increased opportunity, for many Americans, the future typically has been scripted.

The above describes an increasingly bygone era. Instead, given our transition from the manufacturing age to the high technology information age merging into a global economy, with the job losses and the far-reaching consequences of those losses, the future for many Americans has become dynamic, changing, unpredictable, and unscripted. The uncertainties experienced by students are exacerbated by lessening national investment in public higher education, and the accompanying rising personal financial costs of pursuing a college degree or any post-secondary training. Many of today's students are giving up on home-ownership, calculating that their student loans will substitute as their mortgage for the next 30 years. For the first time in generations, children in the United States are not expected to do as well as their parents (Florida, 2005; Hacker, 2006; Uchitelle, 2006; Warren & Tvagi, 2003).

Meanwhile, some faculty and administrators strive to address these less-defined but very real needs of students who are seeking to fashion their way in the world, by creating new degree programs and pedagogical approaches to student learning. In his discussion of the "flat world" and the implications for U.S. education, Friedman (2006) provides help for educators by identifying necessary skills for work in a changing global environment. Recognizing that fundamental transferable cross-disciplinary skills must be developed, Friedman (pp. 302–306) specifies four prime skills and attitudes for success in the 21st century: Learning how to learn; Having passion and curiosity; Playing well with others; and Nurturing the right brain.

- "Learning how to learn." Given the rapid changes that face our students in a knowledge-based information age, it is imperative that they learn how to learn—from books, coursework, training programs, other people who are in a variety of roles, personal and professional experience, and all reliable sources of information. The love of learning and knowing how to learn is not a luxury, but a mandate for the future;
- "Having passion and curiosity." Asking the next question, discovering something new, making new connections and interconnections, sensing the urgency in developing new arenas for opportunities—all of these attributes feed the love of learning and are vital to opening up vistas of opportunity creation;
- "Playing well with others." Sharpening one's people skills, including the ability to relate to people across boundaries, borders, and differences; valuing diversity and cultures with the passion and curiosity to learn from the wisdom of their ages—these skills are helpful to any work and professional advancement, but are seen as absolute essentials for the "flat world'; and
- "Nurturing the right-brain." The right-brain deals with the less defined areas that Friedman terms: "context, emotional expression, and synthesis" (p. 306). While the linear-oriented left-brain remains enormously useful, the right-brain, which is creative, makes con-

nections, sees the big picture, and is able to create opportunities, is clearly an essential component of the skill-set for the future.

While Friedman's prime skills and attitudes can enhance one's success in the context of the American script, it is important to recognize that these attributes typically have been underemphasized in the U.S. educational system. For instance, academic programs often emphasize quantitative methods over people skills; elementary schools frequently find their arts budgets cut, as creative arts programs are seen as electives. Friedman's advice to educators now is to focus on the development of these typically underemphasized skills and attitudes, as they are no longer optional, but are necessary for finding one's way in the workforce of the future.

As Friedman and others point out, on the worldwide scale, the dynamism coupled with lack of script spells opportunity to engage proactively in the global change process. Global citizenship recognizes that the world is being created anew with its myriad of linked interdependencies, and that as global citizens, we need to be empowered with the necessary leadership skills to help us shape an equitable and just world for all—not simply for the privileged few. Tools for the task of advancing global citizenship include developing intellectual capital with a fundamental knowledge base and a commitment to make life better for all people, regardless of continent. In this interconnected age, it is increasingly difficult for any grim futures of some people of the world not to impact all people everywhere.

SERVICE-eLEARNING AND THE UNSCRIPTED FUTURE

As we have seen, in contrast to the expected scripted future, exemplified in the U.S. by the American script, people are faced with an increasingly Unscripted Future. Turning now to the Unscripted Future, DiPadova-Stocks (2008, p. 92) describes that it exhibits the following:

1. Vast unprecedented social, economic, employment, environmental, technological and global changes affecting citizens and the world.
2. Changes so unique and wide-ranging that researchers may have no data for how to assess their impacts or how to deal with them.
3. Changes that are beyond partisan politics.
4. Changes bringing about increased perception of personal and global impact or even risk.

In preparing learners to thrive in a world of change, an adaptive and dynamic model such as *service-eLearning* is appropriate. In an effort to better understand, prepare, and equip learners, we address each characteristic of the Unscripted Future, in turn, below.

The dynamism and unpredictability of the vast changes in the world require people to be able to analyze critically the context in which they are functioning and to determine appropriate action. Service-learning experiences have long assisted students in this regard by placing them into unfamiliar settings and circumstances of which they have to make sense, analyze the situation, and craft productive responses that support other people. Learning technologies and the formation of eLearning communities open the possibilities for the benefits of international exposure, of connecting with people in other cultures and other parts of the world. As is evident, this description reflects Friedman's conceptualization of necessary skills and attitudes, as students learn to play well with others as well as draw on their right-brain attributes. A properly framed *service-eLearning* experience has the potential to add the much needed global, cultural, and international perspectives to the context and to the sense-making required of the student learner.

Turning to the unprecedented nature of the vast changes described in the first characteristic of the Unscripted Future, the second characteristic points to the fact that there may be no data available for measuring and evaluating the impacts of these changes, no frameworks for interpreting the changes, and that our existing paradigms, based on now outdated realities may not work anymore. Predictions are compromised. This in turn points to the little content-specific research base of strategies regarding how to address these changes.

Obviously, disciplinary knowledge and frameworks were largely created in a more familiar time for most of us. As people find themselves changing careers multiple times during their working lives, and as their personal prospects and events around the globe seem more unpredictable, typical academic degrees can become less relevant and increasingly outdated for their lives. In making sense of events around them, they come to rely less on traditional job-specific knowledge and more on their personal experience. They become their own researchers, and given modern technology, they can research from the comfort of their living rooms and laptops. Skills for collecting data, evaluating information, and identifying promising practices become indispensable as everyone becomes his/her own personal reference librarian. Multiple career changes are requiring mastery of an array of transferable skills and competencies.

Clearly Friedman's mandates to learn how to learn and to develop passion and curiosity play a vital role in confronting this characteristic of the Unscripted Future. Skills needed to address this characteristic include cross-disciplinary knowledge, or knowledge not limited to one field, as well as creativity and curiosity—the thirst for new knowledge (because relevant knowledge is being created now at rapid speed and comes to us before it is categorized into academic frameworks) and creative problem-solving skills regarding how the knowledge connects to other arenas and situations.

Like service-learning, *service-eLearning* experiences place students in real-time, real-life situations where they must make sense of the unfamiliar and forge a positive human impact, providing them with a rich arena for nurturing the right-brain and for transferable skill development. This experience alone creates knowledge for the learner, and connects it to other learning. Learning technologies add speed to the time required to research any contextual variables needed in the sense-making process, aiding learning and application. These technologies also can place students having similar experiences into groups, fostering group reflection and shared learning across cultural and international boundaries, thereby forming eLearning communities.

The third characteristic of the Unscripted Future is that the changes involved are clearly beyond borders, location, time, countries, and partisan politics. The changes are independent of political interpretations and political systems—they are driven by massive global and technological forces. Current political systems around the world have the potential to end nuclear weapons, but not the potential to end an array of massive forces, from technology to droughts.

In this global environment, creative global citizenship is required in order to address forces that may so profoundly affect us and the world. Such citizenship is not bound by nationality, not bound by differences and borders, but bound by the keen recognition that forces in one part of the world affect events in other parts of the world.

Again, learning technologies added to service-learning enlarges one's world by propelling the understanding of an intricately connected global environment. *Service-eLearning* functions to bring issues to our attention and to foster creative problem-solving skills within the context of our collective responsibility to act for the common good and for the advancement of human dignity worldwide.

The final characteristic is that awareness of these components of the Unscripted Future brings the very real sense of personal and global impacts due to these forces, as well as personal consequences and risk. Dealing with this aspect of our definition, it is clear that people need to draw on their right-brain functions, as Friedman suggests, and reflect on the issues at hand and how they might be affected. In addition, the development of empathic skills allows projections of how others might be affected by the vast changes that surround us. Problem-solving skills are developed as people seek to proactively address the issues raised in the Unscripted Future, for themselves and for others.

A GENERATION OF LEARNERS FACING
AN UNSCRIPTED FUTURE

Engaged in learning during a time when the current frame and mental model of the world are in flux, learners are struggling to balance the expectations of the American script, (inherited from their parents and historical societal norms, paired with unbounded opportunity), and the reality of preparing for the Unscripted Future. The symbiotic relationship between knowledge and vast change has created a new generation of learners, who are both transformed by and transforming the world around us.

The current generation of learners facing this Unscripted Future at large has already been impacted by vast change and technology and thus approach learning from a different and integrated perspective. "A growing body of evidence reveals that today's college and university students have developed new attitudes and aptitudes as a result of their environment" (Oblinger, 2003, p. 44). Technology is a way of life for these learners, delivering almost instantaneous opportunities for entertainment, to socialize with others, for learning, and consumerism. Learners now possess the ability to allow their individual interests and passions to direct their learning agenda, with immediate access to, and interaction with, resources worldwide. As such, they are predisposed to embrace the *service-eLearning* pedagogical approach of knowledge construction, which is characteristic of autonomous, nonlinear learning.

Because of their ability to easily connect with others worldwide as they buy, learn, and socialize online, this new generation of learners is more aware of the interconnectedness of all people and nations. They are particularly cognizant of the information, experts, peers and global perspective in the limitless environment which extends beyond the four walls of a classroom. Their interactive understanding of the world leads to their conviction toward becoming a global citizen, and the passion to transfer their knowledge toward application for the greater good.

Although this new generation of learners takes advantage of the knowledge-based, technological age we occupy, it is critical to acknowledge that "information is not instruction" (Merrill, 1998, p. 25). Learners still require the guidance and development of empathy, critical reflection, problem-solving skills, adaptability, and most important, how to apply their learning to transform their world. Through *service-eLearning*, educators have the opportunity to help learners decipher, interpret and make value judgments about information, applying their knowledge via civic engagement and meaningful experiences.

Fortunately, the very nature, purpose, and inherent goals of *service-eLearning* uniquely position it to equip the new generation of learners with necessary skills for the "flat world" (Friedman, 2006) and for shaping the

Unscripted Future. Table 10.1 provides a conceptual linkage between the dispositions developed through *service-eLearning,* as elaborated in Chapter 1 of this volume, and the four skills proposed by Friedman (2006). While we acknowledge the interrelated nature and potential overlap of these categories, the chart below represents the most salient corollaries.

Note that *service-eLearning* proportionally responds to Friedman's (2006) challenge with a pedagogical approach designed to foster transferable dispositions. In addition, the learner dispositions developed in *service-eLearning* clearly assists students in addressing the vast unprecedented changes that surround us. For example, problem solving, critical thinking and analysis, and peer learning assist in the sense-making process as learners take in new data and configure those data into valid actionable rationales. Also, global connectedness propels students into perspectives well beyond their immediate environment. Civic responsibility, empathy and other right-

TABLE 10.1 Service-eLearning Pedagogy and Friedman's "Flat World"

Friedman's Skills for a "Flat World"	Service-eLearning Pedagogy and Learner Dispositions
"Learning how to learn"	Non-Linear Paths to Learning
	Dispositions developed: • Self-directed learning • Adaptability • Critical Thinking and Analysis • Problem-solving • Reflection
"Playing well with others"	Peer Learning
	Dispositions developed: • Collaborative exchange • Communication (both written and verbal) • Perspective transformation • Conflict resolution
"Having passion and curiosity"	Global Connectedness
	Dispositions developed: • Personal interest in global social issues • Cross-cultural understanding • Ability to forge connections
"Nurturing the Right Brain"	Application
	Dispositions developed: • Empathy • Civic responsibility • Synthesis • Commitment to human dignity • Creativity • Holistic thinking

brained attitudes assist students in dealing the real and implied risk of the changes they face. Clearly *service-eLearning* offers a promising pedagogy for addressing the challenges of intense learning in such a dynamic time. As higher education approaches the abyss of shifting paradigms needed to embrace rapid change, *service-eLearning* holds great promise.

MOVING FORWARD

We as leaders in higher education approach the ambiguous task of preparing learners for their role in shaping an Unscripted Future. It is imperative to understand the impact our "flattening world" has on current learners, its interconnectedness with knowledge construction, and the transferable skills needed to thrive in a world of change.

A little over a decade ago, the service-learning movement in higher education called on all faculty, whether or not they used service-learning, to reconsider the value and benefit of their current teaching methods—the lecture method, the case-study method, the group method, or other preferred methods. Much more recently, with the increase in technological advances and in learning technologies, attention is drawn to how students learn and the challenges of framing technologies for those who are growing up in the "social-networking era," with access and connectedness in the palm of their hands at all times.

We can no longer rely on traditional teaching and learning models to engage a new generation of learners facing an Unscripted Future. While we tackle the larger issue before us—finding ways for higher education to prepare students shaping that future—the immediate issue addressed by this volume centers on ways in which *service-eLearning* helps educators to prepare students for such uncertainties. As educators, we must help learners develop the skills necessary to shape the new paradigm of the future—uncertainty that is driven by rampant change.

We have considered here the immense challenges of the Unscripted Future and how to educate learners for shaping it, for learning from it, and for global citizenship. Paradigms based on old knowledge are changing and will continue to be challenged by our students' experiences and by accelerating events. Just as we now have Superbugs that are resistant to antibiotics, and economic indicators that were accurate for the past economy but flawed with regards to assessing a global one, we as educators in all fields are called upon to reconsider our traditional disciplinary assumptions and how new frameworks might be developed. *Service-eLearning* invites us on this journey.

NOTE

The authors are indebted to Dr. John Jumara of Park University and to Don Wise, Hauptmann School Fellow, for their helpful review and feedback on this manuscript.

CHAPTER 11

SERVICE-eLEARNING BEST PRACTICES

Possibilities for Engagement

Emily Donnelli-Sallee and Amber Dailey-Hebert

In their study of eLearning's role in the changing landscape of higher education, Marion Coomey and John Stephenson (2001) conclude that "[a]daptive and transformative pedagogy may be the greatest challenge and the true future of higher education and the learner will be at the core" (p. 50). *Service-eLearning* is one such "adaptive and transformative pedagogy." As the chapters in this collection demonstrate, *service-eLearning*, like its parent pedagogies, involves a radical departure from traditional paradigms in re-envisioning and recasting the roles of teacher and taught and the context in which those roles are enacted.

In this chapter, we offer principles and best practices for *service-eLearning* as integrated pedagogy after a brief review of foundational work. Our purpose is to aid in the design of *service-eLearning* experiences to prepare students for what Laurie N. DiPadova-Stocks (2008, p. 132) describes an increasingly "unscripted" future. We wish to underscore, however, that these best practices signify only the first steps toward defining and envisioning a

Service-eLearning: Educating for Citizenship, pages 119–129
Copyright © 2008 by Information Age Publishing
119

pedagogy of *service-eLearning.* As more practitioners share their experiences and insights about the integration of eLearning and service-learning pedagogies, these best practices must be tested, revised, and expanded.

FOUNDATIONAL BEST PRACTICES
FOR SERVICE-LEARNING AND eLEARNING

In approaching best practices for the emergent field of *service-eLearning,* we draw upon existing guidelines developed in both the service-learning and eLearning fields. Both fields place particular value on communication among constituents in the learning process and the repositioning of faculty and students as co-learners. The continuities between these fields' pedagogical values reinforce their potential for productive integration and pave the way for this new learning model. Further, as Amy Kenworthy U'Ren found in her review of the *Michigan Journal of Community Service Learning,* there is much opportunity for dialogue about eLearning, as only two of 155 articles from 1996–2005 addressed the use of eLearning as tool or pedagogy.

Service-Learning Best Practices

Among the best practices developed to guide service-learning, Jeffrey Howard's (1993) "Principles of Good Practice for Service-Learning Pedagogy" remains influential, in particular his first, now axiom "academic credit is for learning, not for service" (p. 3). Howard's principles respond to enduring concerns about integrating community service and disciplinary outcomes while maintaining academic rigor. To that end, he emphasizes the importance of establishing clear disciplinary learning objectives; developing students' readiness and ability to learn from community contexts; creating sound criteria and resources to surround the service experience; and, singularly important, "re-norming" the traditional classroom to privilege active learners and faculty who cannot only transmit knowledge but also co-construct it (pp. 3–12).

Recent studies of technology in service-learning reflect one particular recommendation forwarded by Howard (1993): His observation of the variability in student learning outcomes that can result from heterogeneous service placements and field experiences. This variability becomes even more prominent as service-learning makes its way into information literacy realms, changing the nature and scope of the field. For instance, a recent report on the status of Drake and Iowa University's collaborative project to assess the impact of service-learning on fostering "digital citizenship" concluded that "Service-learning is tough sledding not because the principles are elusive, but rather because the practice is vexing and incremental, placing high demands on the students, faculty, and broader community..." (Schulman et al., 2002, p. 6). The authors note that two principles remain foundational in any implementation of service-learning: reflection and reciprocity. These principles of practice mediate the increasing diversity of service-learning pedagogies and sites, as well as the new challenges presented as traditional face-to-face components are transferred to virtual environments. Reflection remains a key mechanism through which students can utilize a disciplinary framework to understand their service experience and envision future civic action, while reciprocity underscores the critical role of the community partner in determining outcomes for learning in and with the community.

eLearning Best Practices

eLearning best practices echo many of the pedagogical values of service-learning in their response to traditional educational paradigms. Perhaps the most seminal set of eLearning best practices remains Arthur W. Chickering and Stephen C. Ehrmann's (1996) "Implementing the Seven Principles: Technology as Lever." The authors frame the AAHE "Seven Principles for Good Practice in Undergraduate Education" (1987) in the context of technology-mediated learning. That Chickering and Ehrmann based their work on these original principles was a significant step toward recognizing eLearning as not merely technology but pedagogy. Like the foundational principles of service-learning, excellence in eLearning relies on positioning the learner in an active role. They emphasize this in pedagogical practices that ensure faculty-student and student-student communication, as well as continual, formative feedback to help students assess their own learning. Also akin to service-learning best practices, effective eLearning can fuel experiential learning and tap into diverse learning styles and preferences not responsive to traditional pedagogies: "Technological resources can ask for different methods of learning through powerful visuals and well-organized print; through direct, vicarious, and virtual experiences; and through tasks requiring analysis, synthesis, and evaluation, with applications to real-life situations. They can encourage self-reflection and self-evaluation. They can drive collaboration and group problem solving. Technologies can help students learn in ways they find most effective and broaden their repertoires for learning" (Chickering & Ehrmann, 1996, para. 27).

A more recent best practice framework reinforces that eLearning pedagogies, like service-learning, engender active learning and require a de-centered faculty role. Coomey and Stephenson (2001) surveyed the literature on various approaches to online learning to identify four features common to eLearning best practice: dialogue, involvement, support, and control. Dialogue and involvement, they argue, cannot be assumed in online pedagogy—that is, the presence of asynchronous and synchronous communication tools is necessary but insufficient to ensure active learning. Structure, which includes defined questions, multiple paths for inquiry, and timely and consistent moderation, must be present not only in initial course design but throughout the learning process (p. 39). Support from faculty, tutors, and technology specialists ensures that students are prepared for and successful undertaking the self-directed and, in many cases, self-paced learning expected online (pp. 39–40). Finally, control "refers to the extent to which learners have control of key learning activities and the extent to which the learner is encouraged to exercise that control" (p. 40). This control must move beyond the freedom to choose among predetermined discussion prompts or assignments to co-constructing learning outcomes, pursuing individual learning goals, and determining methods and resources for inquiry (pp. 41–48). This range of control reinforces eLearning as "learner-managed learning" (p. 48), and it suggests a range of ways that faculty are de-centered in eLearning pedagogies.

PRINCIPLES AND BEST PRACTICES FOR INTEGRATED PEDAGOGIES: SERVICE-eLEARNING

The established best practices presented above serve as a necessary framework for *service-eLearning* experiences, emphasizing the communication, collaboration, active learning, and de-centered faculty role common to both service-learning and eLearning. However, integrating these two pedagogies requires more than simply drawing on existing best practices. As a new learning model, *service-eLearning* presents unique opportunities and challenges to be negotiated. Thus, we offer three broad principles of *service-eLearning*—inclusion, reflection, and sustainability—each yielding best practices.

Principle One: Inclusion

The principle of inclusion refers to knowledge construction informed by a variety of sources (learners, faculty, and community partners) and to the necessity of creating avenues to support such inclusion.

Best practice reflects integrated disciplinary, civic, and technological learning outcomes. Service-learning starts with the question of how to best teach course content, integrating service as a means to extend disciplinary outcomes in an applied context and to connect those outcomes to issues relevant to civic engagement. Critical to the success of service-learning are clear outcomes that reflect not only academic competencies but the dispositions fostered by service. *Service-eLearning* adds to this equation learning outcomes related to the ways in which technology is used by learners within and outside the academy. Sandra Hill and Christopher Harris demonstrate how *service-eLearning*'s integrated outcomes prepare learners for competent and ethical professional communication, a critical skill in the increasingly e-linked global workplace. In determining outcomes for *service-eLearning*, particular attention must be paid to the areas in which these outcomes overlap—that is, the nexus, mediated by technology, of disciplinary knowledge, community exigency, and individual action.

Best practice involves faculty, students and community partners in the design of service-eLearning. Effective *service-eLearning* necessitates the collaboration of learners, faculty, and community partners in determining, monitoring, and assessing integrated learning outcomes. Kenworthy-U'Ren's inclusive methodology speaks to the importance and reward of involving all key stakeholders. Multidimensional knowledge is a feature of *service-eLearning*, emphasizing collaborative relationships and the positioning of participants as co-learners.

Devising *service-eLearning* curricula must be a shared endeavor starting with assessment of both the university and community partners' goals and capacities for eLearning. As Randy Stoecker, Amy Hilgendorf and Elizabeth Tryon's work highlights, the university must look to the community partner to set the tone for technology incorporation in the *service-eLearning* experience. Although most universities possess myriad eLearning tools for collaborative exchange (course management platforms that allow a guest user, audio and video streaming, virtual whiteboards, and discussion areas), community organizations may not have the hardware, time, or desire to partner through these technologies. Key is a learning plan that considers the resources and goals of the university and community partner to determine the extent to which the latter can be involved in formal components of *service-eLearning*. The most important of those components is reflection (see Post in this collection for a discussion of the benefits of continual and inclusive communication among *service-eLearning* constituents).

Principle Two: Reflection

This principle underscores the critical role of reflection in creating new knowledge, transforming perspective, and equipping global civic engagement.

Best practice engages learners through technology in both individual and collaborative reflection to reach learning outcomes. A unifying thread throughout the work in this volume emphasizes reflection as a main area in which eLearning facilitates student learning gains relevant to changing definitions of content "mastery." These changing definitions are summarized in Peter Schilling's (2005) conclusion that "[w]hat it means to master a field of study has changed. Rather than developing an encyclopedic knowledge of all literature on a single topic, today's students need to know how to find, evaluate, and contextualize information in numerous, different formats on more interdisciplinary topics, but they also need to know how to locate and use the underlying data as well as the technology to sort and present it" (para. 25). Kristine Hoover, Maureen Casile and Ralph Hanke's study asserts the relationship of discussion board reflection to critical thinking and disciplinary knowledge. Their findings also support inclusive design that recognizes patterns of usage across populations and between genders. Christopher Blackwell's students used discussion board reflection not only to frame issues of disciplinary content (in this case therapeutic care) but also to understand community needs (hospice service). His experience extends the disciplinary benefits of Web-mediated discussion to include nurturing empathetic reasoning and basic respect for others.

Further, *service-eLearning* can allow a process wherein individual reflection, while remaining paramount, is complemented by social reflection where faculty, learners, and community partners come together in threaded discussions, blogs, wikis, chatrooms, and other communication tools. This aspect of eLearning supports the critical goal of reciprocity in service-learning by enabling constituents to collaboratively reflect; to define and co-construct new knowledge about issues of shared concern; and to develop strategies for partnering to address those issues. Individual and social reflection enabled and archived by eLearning can be used to assess *service-eLearning* (see Strait's "Levels of Reflection" rubric for one example of leveraging reflection as an assessment indicator).

Best practice promotes metalearning that leads to transformative action. Metacognition, here called "metalearning," is defined as "higher order thinking that involves active control over the cognitive processes engaged in learning" (Livingston, 2003, p. 1). Hypermedia learning environments, which by their nature are nonlinear, activate metalearning by requiring learners to exercise more control over the content and their processes for acquiring knowledge (Schwartz et al., 2004). This metalearning is fostered by *service-eLearning* reflection mechanisms that archive individual reflection and group discussions so that recurrent issues, themes, and action plans can be identified (see Post; Stoecker, Hilgendorf & Tryon in this collection for a discussion of the value of archived material in promoting substantive participation and deeper levels of reflection and action).

The ability to function within these hypermedia environments is emerging as a requisite skill for individual citizens to undertake transformative action about issues that matter to them. For example, blogs and other forms of online social networking increasingly serve as primary venues for citizens to exercise watch over policy making. George Washington University's Institute for Politics, Democracy, and the Internet recently published research about the role of social networking software, in particular the ways in which "blogs may be altering the way politics is practiced and policy is developed, particularly among offices which regularly read blogs and/or already assist in running or participating in blogs" (Sroka, 2006, p. 29). *Service-eLearning* can tap the kinds of metalearning engendered by eLearning to equip students for new kinds of civic engagement.

Principle Three: Sustainability

The principle of sustainability refers to the infrastructures necessary to provide practical support to faculty, learners, and community partners; to undertake research and assessment; and to create local, national and international networks to sustain *service-eLearning.*

Best practice builds diverse communities of inquiry across disciplinary and geographical boundaries. *Service-eLearning* sustainability is supported by communities of inquiry that transcend disciplinary and geographical boundaries. As Hilary E. Kahn, Sarah M. Stelzner, Mary E. Riner, Armando E. Soto-Rojas, Joan Henkle, M. Humberto A. Veras Godoy, José L. Antón de la Concha, and E. Angeles Martínez-Mier in this collection found, eLearning has immense potential to expand the reach of service-learning to interdisciplinary and international realms. Kahn and others specifically noted that sustained communication among constituents facilitated relationships— between students and faculty from different disciplines and institutions, as well as between institutions and community partners.

Interdisciplinary and international learning takes on particular importance when we consider the needs of today's student learners. Laurie N. DiPadova-Stocks and Amber Dailey-Hebert assert that transferable skills are critical to functioning within new paradigms for learning and working. These skills are developed out of creative and integrative thinking not confined by disciplinary boundaries and not limited by geography. They argue that cross-cultural understanding is one such disposition enabled by *service-eLearning*'s global opportunities.

Best practice involves continual and multidimensional assessment to foster sustainability over time. Continual feedback and input from all key stakeholders are necessary to revise and improve practice. Also critical to the sustainability of *service-eLearning* is research comparing service-learning experiences facilitated with and without eLearning pedagogies. In the Hamline University experience, Jean Strait presents one such assessment model to measure student learning gains through input from students, faculty and community partners involved. This assessment, Strait notes, has resulted in the continuation of academic and community partnerships and the development of new and expanded service- eLearning opportunities. Strait's experience underscores the critical relationship of assessment to reciprocity to sustainability across time.

SYNTHESIS: SUGGESTED FEATURES
OF SERVICE-eLEARNING COURSES

The principles and best practices reviewed above provide guideposts for practitioners interested in pursuing *service-eLearning*. Successful *service-eLearning* requires an inclusive process that involves all constituents—student learners, community partners, faculty—in planning, implementation, and assessment. *Service-eLearning* courses must be anchored by integrated outcomes and must include assessment measures that gauge discipline-based and transferable skills and competencies. Multiple avenues for individual and communal reflection allow participants to construct new knowledge. The extent to which eLearning is integrated as a delivery modality has a direct impact on the geographic and cultural diversity of the learners and consequently the range of local, national and even global models for technology-mediated democracy that emerge.

GUIDING QUESTIONS FOR SERVICE-eLEARNING
STUDENTS, FACULTY, AND COMMUNITY PARTNERS

Constituents involved in *service-eLearning* experiences must possess the ability to work within eLearning pedagogical frameworks to complete the components of service-learning (for instance, reflection and service with communities). Here we provide an overview of some of the guiding questions that may serve as a helpful starting point for the development of *service-eLearning* experiences that feature inclusion, reflection, and sustainability.

Students

Service-eLearning students, especially those who will be geographically removed from their faculty, must possess knowledge of their local communities and the opportunities for engagement within those communities. They must understand the capacity for the self-directed yet collaborative learning needed for success in online environments and beyond. And they must evaluate their technology access as well as their experiences and ability to learn with and through technology. *Service-eLearning* involves scenarios and situations that challenge or expose flaws in existing paradigms and that prompt us to act upon newly found understanding. Negotiating these "expectation failures" (Bain, 2004) is one function of reflection, and students considering eLearning should assess their comfort level engaging in this kind of self-analysis online.

Faculty

It is important for faculty to engage in similar kinds of reflection to determine their fit with *service-eLearning* approaches. These faculty must have the knowledge and desire to enact eLearning as both venue and pedagogy, just as they must be able to involve the community partner as a co-participant in the instruction of integrated learning outcomes. A de-centered faculty role is critical to joining in reflective activities with students and community partners in the online environment. In determining the best use of technology in *service-eLearning*, faculty are tasked with understanding and negotiating the expectations the expectations and resources of learners, community partners, and, in some cases, the populations represented by those community partners. Finally, faculty are compelled to consider their ability to ensure flexibility and responsiveness to *service-eLearning* constituents, often distanced from each other geographically, within eLearning's 24/7 environment. Both formative and summative assessment, involving multiple perspectives, supports reciprocity and sustainability in *service-eLearning*.

Community Partners

Like faculty, community partners must consider how agency-based learning outcomes can integrate with disciplinary and technology objectives. It is critical to determine what parameters surrounding technology resource, access, and appropriate use will affect the design of the *service-eLearning* experience. As *service-eLearning* grows so will the call for community partners willing to oversee service experiences facilitated partially or wholly online. Few models representing this kind of university and community partnership exist. Community partners will be called upon to identify what sites, physical and virtual, are available to students for service experiences, recognizing the technical and time requirements to facilitate fully online service experiences with students. To that end, community partners should reflect on the extent which they can serve as co-facilitators of the learning experience, participating in reflective activities with student and faculty constituents.

We conclude this section with a visual synthesis[1] (Figure 11.1) of key guiding questions for the design of *service-eLearning* experiences. This visual can serve as heuristic for students, faculty, and community partners to initiate and structure conversations about the unique components of *service-eLearning*.

INTEGRATING KNOWLEDGE AND RESOURCES
FOR SUSTAINABLE SERVICE-eLEARNING

Lori Vogelgesang (2004) is one of many who recognize that successful implementation of service-learning requires institutional support, including fit with institutional mission, adaptability of curricular structures, and adequateness of resources. The same holds true for *service-eLearning*. Underlying the recommendations presented here is the recognition that faculty embarking on this creative, rigorous, and intellectually demanding endeavor need institutional support from their presidents, provosts, and deans. This support is twofold: First, academic leaders must ensure communication and collaboration between campus service-learning offices/centers and eLearning programs. Just as *service-eLearning* involves the integration of two pedagogies, it also implies the merging of resources to support those pedagogies, including the development of new structures. Second, this support should recognize *service-eLearning* as intellectual inquiry by making provisions for professional development, research assistance, and reward via promotion and tenure processes.

To understand and embrace shifting paradigms in higher education, it is critical to acknowledge the new generation of learners and the symbiotic relationship between their learning and technology. "Not only do our students possess skills and experiences that previous generations do not, but the very neurological structures and pathways they have developed as part of their learning are based on the technologies they use to create, store, and disseminate information" (Schilling, 2005, para. 1). As these learners use technology to seek connectedness and find purpose in a rapidly changing world, *service-eLearning* presents a dynamic and responsive pedagogy. The inclusive nature of *service-eLearning* unites all stakeholders to transcend traditional paradigms and propel this new learning model forward.

NOTE

1. We are indebted to Rena M. Palloff and Keith Pratt's (2003) "Elements of a high quality online course or program" as it served as a visual/conceptual model that influenced our own.

Service-eLearning Partners

- What sites, physical and virtual, are available to students for service experiences in my organization and community?
- To what extent do I have the resources to be a continuous partner, co-learning with students and co-instructing with faculty?
- Am I available to engage in reflective activities with student and faculty constituents?
- What parameters surround technology resources, access, and appropriate use that could affect my participation in service-eLearning?

Service-eLearning Curriculum

- How does the curriculum integrate assessment measures for disciplinary, civic, and eLearning outcomes?
- Does the curriculum provide opportunities to explore technology's emergent role in shaping democracy?
- Does the curriculum include multiple mechanisms for individual and collaborative reflection?
- Is the curriculum flexible enough to adapt to changing learner and community partner needs?

Service-eLearning Students

- Do I have knowledge of my communities and the opportunities for service within them?
- Am I willing to examine and challenge my own assumptions to reach a broader understanding?
- Am I willing to reflect, often collaboratively and in writing, about my own thinking as student and citizen?
- Do I posses the skills necessary to learn within non-linear, self-directed online environments?

Service-eLearning Faculty

- What beliefs about technology and global citizenship motivate me to undertake service-eLearning and, accordingly, how will I participate as a co-learner?
- What is my level of access, knowledge, and understanding of educational technologies—Am I able to learn with and teach through technology?
- Am I willing to validate the community partner as co-educator?
- Am I prepared to be flexible and responsive to multiple stakeholders within eLearning's 24/7 environment?

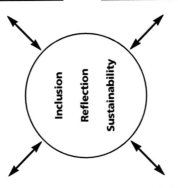

Inclusion
Reflection
Sustainability

Figure 11.1 Guiding questions for undertaking *service-eLearning.*

NEW FRONTIERS AND INSTITUTIONAL COMMITMENTS TO SERVICE-eLEARNING

A Call to Action

Beverley Byers-Pevitts

I look to the future, not to just be a part of it, but to shape it.

—John F. Kennedy, Jr.

From the very beginnings of the United States, education has been regarded as imperative, as necessary for survival. John Adams, Thomas Jefferson and other founders saw the purpose of education to prepare citizens, equipped to shape the future, citizens who could be entrusted with self-governance. They recognized education as the key to ensuring the viability of their "script" (outlined in the founding documents of the nation) for a self-governing society.

The nation and the world stand on the precipice of a new frontier. Today's frontier is not confined by seas or boundaries, by language or culture, or by political institutions. The frontier facing educators is far more daunt-

Service-eLearning: Educating for Citizenship, pages 131–133

ing and interconnects everyone on the planet. It is described in this volume as the Unscripted Future.

Yet today, the education imperative is seriously eroded in the United States, while vigorously embraced in other major economies of the world. All too often, obtaining a degree in higher education is much like purchasing an automobile, regarded as a private gain rather than as a public good vital to society's growth and innovation. Higher education is dangerously out of reach for many in this country; for those who do earn their degrees, mountains of personal debt are often required. Our human intellectual capital is seriously shortchanged; businesses are undermined; and United States' global competitiveness may be compromised in the long-term.

In order to meet the demands of the new frontier, we must relentlessly question ourselves and our practices. The education imperative must be firmly reestablished with inclusion as its centerpiece. Inclusion involves "access to academic excellence which will prepare learners to think critically, communicate effectively and engage in lifelong learning while serving a global community" ("Park University Mission," para. 2).

Inclusion also involves willingness to abandon our long-held presumption of possessing all relevant knowledge, a notion contrary to the traditional academic model. The demands of the Unscripted Future require welcoming knowledge from a variety of sources, including students and community members (see Kenworthy-U'Ren and Donnelli-Sallee & Dailey-Hebert in this collection).

In a 2003 article published in *On the Horizon*, James L. Morrison, Professor Emeritus of Education at the University of North Carolina at Chapel Hill, noted: "In 2020, the landscape of higher education in the US will look very different. . . . The focus of education will be to produce graduates who can use a variety of information technology tools and techniques to access, evaluate, analyze, and communicate information and who can work effectively in teams with people from different ethnic groups. In this way, institutions will better prepare their students to address a wide range of real-world issues and choices, the tidy answers to which are not in the back of a textbook" (para. 23). Morrison's observations challenge us to recognize the limits of our linear structures for learning and creating knowledge, including the confines of the traditional classroom.

eLearning is valuable in offering new models for inclusion and student-led learning. Like many other institutions, Park University serves many other institutions, Park University serves students who take courses in both online and face-to-face formats from multiple locations, locales, desktops, and notebooks around the world. As part of one of the largest online learning programs in the country, Park University students are local, international, military our students are local, national, international, military, and often completing their graduation requirements while on duty in Kuwait, Iraq, Afghanistan, and other nations, but they share the same classroom.

Clearly, eLearning as a technology equips us to meet the needs of these learners, but as a pedagogy, it gives us much more. eLearning paves the way for a curriculum that engenders the global social awareness requisite for an informed citizenry. Part of being a responsible citizen on the global stage is to possess a level of cultural competency, and eLearning makes cultural competence a reality by enabling diverse learners to meet in virtual classrooms facilitated by faculty committed to linking disciplinary content to larger questions of civic responsibility.

As universities undertake eLearning as a pedagogy of global citizenship, service-learning emerges as a synergistic partner. Over the past two decades, service-learning has proven its worth as a pedagogy for engaging citizenship. eLearning builds upon and extends that foundation globally, removing obstacles of geography and, in many cases, homogeneity. With *service-eLearning* as a pedagogy of engagement, student collaborations are limitless, as are the possibilities available within this new educational paradigm.

The future is now being shaped. The question before us is: *Are we providing all that is necessary for shaping a sustainable and livable world?* This is not a call for us to turn from our traditions, our foundational liberal-arts curricula and our historic campuses. In order to shape the future, we must embrace our history to reclaim the education imperative.

We are now in the new frontier, the new world. This frontier is no longer on the shores of Jamestown or in the harsh Massachusetts winter. There is no turning back, no ship to take us back to England. The new frontier is in each technology, in each building, each classroom, each faculty member. At the same time, it is also in every nation of the world and, with technology, in the palms of our hands. Most important, it is in the eyes of our student learners who, at this very moment, are busy creating their own new communities and cultural metalanguages.

As educational leaders, our task is clear. Only by seizing the education imperative can we advance global citizenship and, by extension, shape the future of the planet.

ABOUT THE AUTHORS

José Luis Antón de la Concha, DDS, is the Dean of Academic Affairs of the Health Science Institute of the Universidad Autónoma del Estado de Hidalgo (UAEH) in Pachuca, México. Dr. Antón attended graduate courses in Orthodontics and Educative Technology. Dr. Anton is a member of the Mexican Orthodontist Council, the Orthodontist Association of the Federal District, and the Postgraduate Orthodontist Association of the state of Hidalgo State.

Christopher W. Blackwell, Ph.D., is an Assistant Professor in the College of Nursing at the University of Central Florida in Orlando. He conducts research in health disparities and teaches across the undergraduate and graduate curriculums in community and public health, epidemiology, and advanced practice nursing. Dr. Blackwell also serves as an editorial reviewer for the Journal of Service-learning in Education.

Beverley Byers-Pevitts, Ph.D., is President and CEO of Park University in Parkville, Missouri, and Professor of Communication and Theatre, as well as a professionally produced and published playwright who has had numerous articles published in educational journals and books. Since her arrival in 2001 as the first woman to be named President of Park University, the university budget has increased 123 percent; enrollment has increased 41 percent; and the endowment has grown by 81 percent. She is active locally, nationally and internationally as an outspoken advocate for the proactive role of higher education to develop leaders within our global communities. She has lectured widely on leadership, access and equity in higher education, academic restructuring, faculty roles, distance learning and the future of universities, with a global and virtual emphasis.

Maureen Casile, Ph.D., is an Assistant Professor in the Department of Management at Bowling Green State University. Her areas of interest include business strategy, organization theory, institutional theory, organizational behavior, organizational culture, outsourcing, and privatization.

Amber Dailey-Hebert, Ph.D., is Associate Professor of Education and Director of the Center for Excellence in Teaching and Learning at Park University, where she was recently named Distinguished Faculty Scholar. She has contributed to the field and published research in eLearning effectiveness, teaching best practices, leadership in higher education, and epistemological development.

Laurie N. DiPadova-Stocks, Ph.D., is Professor of Public Administration at Park University and Dean of the Hauptmann School for Public Affairs, where she has launched the Unscripted Future Initiative. As an advocate for the responsibility of universities to communities, she has spoken at national, international, and regional academic conferences on engagement pedagogies and is published in this area. She initiated the Academy of Management's Service-Learning Fellows initiative.

Emily Donnelli-Sallee, Ph.D., is Assistant Professor of English at Park University, where she also serves as Assistant Director of the University's Center for Excellence in Teaching and Learning. Her research examines how public sphere theory can inform civic engagement pedagogies in first-year composition. She has been published in the *Journal of Advanced Composition*, *Academic Exchange Quarterly*, and the *Journal of Educators Online*.

Ralph Hanke, Ph.D., is an Assistant Professor of entrepreneurship and management at Bowling Green State University. His research interests include team creativity, conflict management, entrepreneurship education, and the philosophy of organizing.

Christopher Harris, Ph.D., is Assistant Professor of English at the University of Louisiana at Monroe. His research interests are in composition pedagogy, composition history, teaching and training in online environments, and communication across the curriculum. Recent academic activity includes a grant-funded project to integrate service-learning into ULM Freshmen-Year Seminar, Summer Reading Program and Learning Communities.

Joan Henkle, DNS, RN, is an Assistant Professor of Clinical Public Health for the Department of Public Health (DPH), IU School of Medicine and Manager for Community and Student Affairs. She administers and coordinates the community-based academic experiences for the Master of Public Health (MPH) students and coordinates linkages between her department and public health partners for community assessment and planning activities. She has worked with students in community-based learning projects in Indianapolis, Mexico, and Honduras.

Amy Hilgendorf, is a graduate student at the University of Wisconsin-Madison in the department of Human Development and Family Studies. Previously she served as an AmeriCorps*VISTA with the University of Wisconsin-Extension to guide service-learning and civic engagement initiatives.

Sandra Hill, Ph.D., is Assistant Professor of English at University of Louisiana, Monroe, where she teaches technical writing, composition, and literature. She recently received a service-learning grant from ULS Serves for service projects, is developing the Professional Writing Program at ULM, and was nominated for the 2007 Thomas Ehrlich Faculty Award for Service-Learning.

Kristine F. Hoover, MBA, MOD, is an instructor in the Management Department at Bowling Green State University. Her research interests include service-learning, leadership, strategic human resources, and ethics.

Hilary E. Kahn, Ph.D., is the Associate Director for the Center for the Study of Global Change at Indiana University Bloomington and Adjunct Professor of Anthropology at Indiana University Bloomington and IUPUI. She currently directs an international service-learning and cultural immersion program in Bluefields, Jamaica. She has recently published her first book Seeing and Being Seen: The Q'eqchi' Maya of Guatemala and Beyond.

Amy Kenworthy-U'Ren, Ph.D., is an Associate Professor of management in the Faculty of Business, Technology, and Sustainable Development at Bond University in Queensland, Australia. With over 17 years experience in service-learning, she is considered an expert and has served as guest editor for special issues on service-learning in many of the leading management education journals including the Academy of Management Learning & Education, the International Journal of Case Method Research & Application, the Journal of Management Education, and a forthcoming issue of the International Journal of Organizational Analysis.

E. Angeles Martínez-Mier, DDS, MSD, Ph.D., is Associate Professor at Indiana University School of Dentistry and serves as director of the Fluoride research program and the Binational/Cross-cultural Center for Health Enhancement. She has lectured as an invited speaker throughout the country and abroad, and currently teaches cultural and linguistic effectiveness and preventive dentistry in the DDS and graduate programs and has co-directed the Calnali international Service-Learning Project since 2001.

Susan W. Post, is a graduate student currently pursuing a Ph.D. in Educational Leadership from Touro University International. Research interests are in experiential eLearning with special emphasis in service-learning pedagogy. The research intention for her doctoral dissertation entails service-learning stakeholders' perceptions and beliefs about eLearning technology integration with service-learning practices.

Mary E. Riner, DNS, RN, is Associate Professor and Director of the World Health Organization Collaborating Center in Healthy Cities at Indiana University School of Nursing. She teaches community health nursing in the bachelors, masters, and doctoral programs. As a published author and fellow of the Institute for Action Research in Community Health, Dr. Riner engages in research that involves partnering with local and international communities to address existing problems in a manner that engages the community in identifying health problems and developing and applying solutions.

Armando E. Soto-Rojas, DDS, MPH, is Assistant Professor at Indiana University School of Dentistry (IUSD) and has had academic appointments at the Universidad Intercontinental, Guy's Hospital in London, England, at the Consejo Nacional de Información y Prevención del SIDA in Mexico City and at the Instituto Nacional de Ciencias Médicas y Nutrición Salvador Zubirán, in Mexico City. He was awarded a Boyer Scholars fellowship in 2006 by the IUPUI Center for Service and Learning. Since 2004 he has co-directed the IUSD Calnali International Service-Learning Project.

Sarah M. Stelzner, MD, is Co-Principal Investigator on the Partnerships for Change-Dyson and Anne Dyson Community Pediatrics Training Initiatives. She directs the Community I and II rotations and co-directs the Calnali International Service-Learning Project, a multi-disciplinary program that partners with health providers in Mexico. She teaches cultural and linguistic effectiveness and serves as co-Legislative Liaison for the Indiana Chapter of the American Academy of Pediatrics.

Randy Stoecker, Ph.D., is Associate Professor in the Department of Rural Sociology at the University of Wisconsin, with a joint appointment in the University of Wisconsin—Extension Center for Community and Economic Development. He has written extensively on community organizing and development and community-based research including the books Defending Community, Research Methods for Community Change, and the co-authored book Community-Based Research in Higher Education.

Jean Strait, Ph.D., is Associate Professor of Education at Hamline University. She was recruited as the first Director of Faculty Development for a state Campus Compact.

Elizabeth Tryon, is a Community Partner Specialist with the Human Issues Program at Edgewood College. She coordinates service-learning opportunities for students at community organizations, and collaborates with faculty and others to develop opportunities for students' service-based graduation requirement.

M. Humberto A. Veras Godoy, MSc, is the Dean of the Health Science Institute of the Universidad Autónoma del Estado de Hidalgo (UAEH) in Pachuca, Mexico and the previous Dean of the Medical School, Director of the Academic Exchange Office and General sub-secretary of the Universidad Autónoma del Estado de Hidalgo. He is the President of the Asociación Mexicana de Facultades y Escuelas de Medicina (Mexican Association of Faculties and Medical Schools) from 2003–2007, and a member of the General Hospital Council G.A Gonzalez in Mexico City.

Edward Zlotkowski, Ph.D, is a national voice in service-learning, and has contributed to the proliferation of service-learning programs in U.S. higher education through his writing, editing, and organizing activities. A much sought after conference speaker, he is a professor of English at Bentley College where in 1990 he founded the Bentley Service-Learning Center. He writes and speaks extensively on a wide range of service-learning and engagement-related topics, serving as general editor of the American Association for Higher Education's 21-volume series on service-learning in the academic disciplines, and numerous additional books and articles. He has designed and facilitated professional development opportunities in service-learning for provosts and deans as well as summer institutes for engaged academic departments. A consultant with the Corporation on National Service, Campus Compact (as Senior Faculty Fellow), the Council of Independent Colleges, the Pew Charitable Trusts, and with regional and state service-learning associations from Maine to Hawaii, he has also worked with several hundred individual colleges and universities at home and abroad.

REFERENCES

About Hamline. Retrieved June 18, 2007, from Hamline University Web site: http://www.hamline.edu/hamline_info/about_hamline/about_hamline.html

Adobor, H., & Daneshfar, A. (2006). Management simulations: Determining their effectiveness. *Journal of Management Development, 25*(2), 151–168.

American Association of Colleges and Universities (2007). *College learning for the new global century: A report from the National Leadership Council for Liberal Education and America's Promise.* Washington, DC: AAC&U.

American Association of Colleges of Nursing. (2002). *Moving forward with community-based nursing education.* Washington, DC: Author.

Anderson, J. (1998). *Service-learning and teacher education. ERIC Digest* (Report No. EDO-SP-97-1). Washington, DC: ERIC Clearinghouse on Teaching and Teacher Education. (ERIC Document Reproduction Service No. ED421481)

Anderson, T., & Elloumi, F. (Eds.). (2004). *Theory and practice of online learning.* Alberta: Athabasca University.

Aristotle (trans, 1912). *Aristotle's Politics: A treatise on government* (W. Ellis, Trans.). New York: E.P. Dutton.

Ash, S. L., Clayton, P., & Atkinson, M. (2005). Integrating reflection and assessment to capture and improve student learning. *Michigan Journal of Community Service Learning, 11*(2), 49–60.

Ashwill, M. A. (2004). Developing intercultural competence for the masses. *International Educator, 13*(2), 16–25.

Bain, K. (2004). *What the best college teachers do.* Cambridge, MA: Harvard University Press.

Bandura, A. (1977). *Social learning theory.* Englewood Cliffs, NJ: Prentice-Hall.

Barnard, G. (2005, April/May). Why e-learning affects us all. *British Journal of Administrative Management,* 24–25.

Beauchesne, M. A., & Meservey, P. M. (1999). An interdisciplinary community-based educational model. *Journal of Professional Nursing, 15,* 38–43.

Service-eLearning: Educating for Citizenship, pages 141–150

Bennett, G., & Green F. P. (2001). Promoting service learning via online instruction. *College Student Journal, 35,* 491–498.

Bhaerman, R., Gomez, B., & Cordell, K. (1998). *The role of service-learning in educational reform.* Needham Heights, MA: Simon and Schuster Custom Publishing.

Bissonette, R., & Route, C. (1994). The educational effects of clinical rotations in non-industrialized countries. *Family Medicine, 26,* 226–231.

Bjork, O., & Schwartz, J. P. (2005, June 4). *E-service learning: Web writing as community service.* Retrieved February 10, 2007, from: http://kairosnews.org/e-service-learning-web-writing-as-community-service

Blanck, P. D. (1981). Sex differences in eavesdropping on nonverbal cues: Developmental changes. *Journal of Personality & Social Psychology, 41,* 391–396.

Blyth, D., Saito, R., & Berkas, T. (1997). A quantitative study of the impact of service learning programs. In A. Waterman (Ed.), *Service-learning: Applications from the research* (pp. 39–56). Mahwah, NJ: Lawrence Erlbaum.

Bolter, J. D. (1991). *Writing space: The computer, hypertext, and the history of writing.* Hillsdale, NJ: Lawrence Erlbaum.

Bolter, J.D. & Grusin, R. (2002). *Remediation.* Cambridge, MA: MIT Press.

Bowden, M., & Scott, J. B. (2003). *Service-learning in technical and professional communication.* New York: Longman.

Boyle-Baise, M. (1998). Community service learning for multicultural education: An exploratory study with preservice teachers. *Equity and Excellence in Education, 31*(2), 52–60.

Bransford, J. D., Brown, A. L., & Cocking, R. R. (Eds.). (1999). *How people learn: Brain, mind, experience, and school.* Washington, DC: National Academy Press. Retrieved February 20, 2007, from http://www.nap.edu/catalog.php?record_id=6160

Braun, J. A., Jr. (2004). Technology in the classroom: Tools for building stronger communities and better citizens. *Kappa Delta Pi Record, 40*(2), 69.

Bringle, R., & Hatcher, J. A. (1995). A service learning curriculum for faculty. *Michigan Journal of Community Service Learning, 2*(1), 112–122.

Bringle, R. G., & Hatcher, J. A. (1999). Reflection in service learning: Making meaning of experience. *Educational Horizons, 77*(4), 179–185.

Brookfield, S. D. (1987). *Developing critical thinkers: Challenging adults to explore alternative ways of thinking and acting.* San Francisco: Jossey-Bass.

Bushouse, B. K. (2005). Community nonprofit organizations and service-learning: Resource constraints to building partnerships with universities. *Michigan Journal of Community Service Learning, 12*(1), 32–40.

Cairn, R., & Kielsmeier, J. (1991). *Growing hope: A sourcebook on integrating youth service into the school curriculum.* St. Paul, MN: National Youth Leadership Council.

Callister, L. C., & Hobbins-Garbett, D. (2000, May). "Enter to learn, go forth to serve": Service-learning in nursing education. *Journal of Professional Nursing, 16,* 177–183.

Carpenter, P. P., & Roberts, E. (2006). *Wikis work for online tech ed courses.* Retrieved February 10, 2007, from: http://www.techlearning.com/showArticle.php?articleID= 193006217

Carr, S. (2000, July 7). Many professors are optimistic on distance learning, survey finds. *The Chronicle of Higher Education,* p. A35.

Carter-Pokras, O., O'Neill, M. J. F., & Soleras, A. (2004). Provision of linguistically appropriate services to persons with limited English proficiency: A needs and resources investigation. *American Journal of Management Care, 10,* SP29-SP36.

Chalfen, R. (1992). Picturing culture through indigenous imagery: A telling story. In P. I. Crawford & D. Turton (Eds.), *Film as ethnography* (pp. 222–224). Manchester: Manchester University Press.

Chesler, M.A., Kellman-Fritz, J., & Knife-Gould, A. (2003). Training peer facilitators for community service learning leadership. *Michigan Journal of Community Service Learning, 9*(2), 59–76.

Chickering, A.W., & Gamson, Z. (1987). Seven principles of good practice in undergraduate education. *AAHE Bulletin, 39,* 3–7.

Chickering, A., & Ehrmann, S. (1996, October). Implementing the seven principles: Technology as lever [Electronic version]. *AAHE Bulletin,* 3–6.

Colby, A., Ehrlich, T., Beaumont, E., & Stephens, J. (2003). *Educating citizens: Preparing America's undergraduates for lives of moral and civic responsibility.* San Francisco: Jossey-Bass.

Coomey, M., & Stephenson, J. (2001). Online learning: It is all about dialogue, involvement, support and control—according to the research. In Stephenson, J. (Ed.) *Teaching and learning online: Pedagogies for new technologies* (pp. 37–50). Sterling, VA: Stylus.

Creamer, E. G. (1999). Feminist pedagogy in action: An on-line module about service-learning. In M. James-Deramo (Ed.), *Best practices in cyber-serve: Integrating technology with service-learning instruction* (pp. 101–109). Blacksburg, VA: Virginia Tech Service Learning Center.

Curtis, D. D., & Lawson, M. J. (2001). Exploring collaborative online learning. *Journal of Asynchronous Learning Networks, 5*(1), 21–34.

Cruz, N. I., & Giles, D. E. Jr. (2000). Where's the community in service-learning research? [Special issue]. *Michigan Journal of Community Service Learning,* 28–34.

D'Cruz, D. (2003, June). The secret to successful e-learning: Make it social. *Management,* pp. 47–49.

Dewey, J. (1916). *Democracy and education: An introduction to the philosophy of education.* New York: Macmillan.

Dick, B. (2000). *Communication.* Retrieved February 10, 2007, from: http://www.scu.edu.au/ schools/gcm/ar/arp/communicn.html

Dieberger, A., & Guzdial, M. (2003). CoWeb—Experiences with collaborative web spaces. In C. Lueg & D. Fisher (Eds.), *From usenet to cowebs: Interacting with social information spaces* (pp. 155–166). London: Springer.

DiPadova-Stocks, L. N. (2005). Two major concerns about service-learning: What if we don't do it? And what if we do? *Academy of Management Learning & Education, 4,* 345–353.

DiPadova-Stocks, L. N. (2008). Fostering social and civic responsibility by organizations and their people. In C. Wankel (Ed.), *Handbook of 21st century management.* Thousand Oaks, CA: Sage.

Dorado, S., & Giles, D.E., Jr. (2004). Service-learning partnerships: Paths of Engagement. *Michigan Journal of Community Service Learning, 11*(1), 25–37.

Drezner, D., & Farrell, H. (2004). *The power and politics of blogs.* Paper presented at the 2004 meeting of the American Political Science Association.

Drupal. (n.d.). Retrieved February 10, 2007, from: http://www.drupal.org

Dunlap, M. R. (1998). Voices of students in multicultural service-learning settings. *Michigan Journal of Community Service Learning, 5*(1), 58–67.

Dutton, J., Dutton, M., & Perry, J. (2002). How do online students differ from lecture students? *Journal of Asynchronous Learning Networks, 6,* 1–20.

Eby, J. W. (1998). Why service-learning is bad. Retrieved February 10, 2007, from: http://www.messiah.edu/external_programs/agape/service_learning/articles/wrongsvc.pdf

Enos, S., & Morton, K. (2003). Developing a theory and practice of campus-community partnerships. In B. Jacoby & Associates (Eds.), *Building partnerships for service-learning,* (pp. 20–41). San Francisco: John Wiley & Sons.

e107.org. (n.d.). Retrieved February 10, 2007, from: http://www.e107.org/news.php

Ervin, N. E., Bickes, J. T., & Schim, S. M. (2006). Environment of care: A curriculum model for preparing a new generation of nurses. *Journal of Nursing Education, 45,* 75–80.

Eshlemann, J., & Davidhizar, R. (2000). Community assessment: An RN-BSN partnership with community. *Association of Black Nursing Faculty Journal, 11*(2), 28–31.

Eyler, J., & Giles, D. E., Jr. (1997). The importance of reflection in service learning. In A. Waterman (Ed.), *Service-learning: Applications from the research* (pp. 57–76). Mahwah, NJ: Lawrence Erlbaum.

Eyler, J., & Giles, D. E., Jr. (1999). *Where's the learning in service-learning?* San Francisco: Jossey-Bass.

Eyler, J., Giles, D. E., Jr., Lunch, C. & Gray, C. (1997). *Service-learning and the development of reflective judgment.* Paper presented at the American Educational Research Association, Chicago.

Flores, G., Abreu, M., Olivares, M. A., & Kaster, B. (1998). Access barriers to health care for Latino children. *Archives of Pediatric and Adolescent Medicine, 152,* 1119–1125.

Flores, G., & Vega, L. R. (1998). Barriers to health care access for Latino children: A review. *Family Medicine, 30,* 196–205.

Florida, R. (2005). *The Flight of the creative class: The new global competition for talent.* New York: HarperCollins.

Foot, K., & Schneider, S. (2006). *Web campaigning.* Cambridge, MA: MIT Press.

Foundation for Hospital Art. (2003). Retrieved May 10, 2007, from: http://www.hospitalart.com/about_mission.html

Friedman, T. L. (2006). *The world is flat: A brief history of the twenty-first century.* New York: Farrar, Straus and Giroux.

Galvez-Martin, M. E., Bowman, C., & Morrison, M. (1996). *A longitudinal study on reflection of pre-service teachers.* Paper presented at the annual meeting of the Mid-western Educational Research Association, Chicago.

Gassner, L. A., Wotton, K., Clare, J., Hofmeyer, A., & Buckman, J. (1999). Evaluation of a model of collaboration: Academic and clinician in the development and implementation of undergraduate teaching. *Collegian, 6*(3), 14–21.

Gelmon, S. B., Holland, B. A., Driscoll, A., Spring, A., & Kerrigan, S. (2001). *Assessing service-learning and civic engagement: Principles and techniques.* Providence, RI: Campus Compact.

Gelmon, S. B., Holland, B. A., Seifer, S. D., Shinnamon, A., & Connors K. (1998). Community–University partnerships for mutual learning, *Michigan Journal of Community Service Learning, 5*(1), 97–107.

Giles, D., Honnet, E. P., & Migliore, S. (Eds.) (1991). *Research agenda for combining service and learning in the 1990s.* Raleigh, NC: National Society for Experiential Education.

Glaser, B. G., & Strauss, A. L. (1967). *The discovery of grounded theory: Strategies for qualitative research.* Chicago: Aldine.

Gobbo, L., Drake, M., Nieckoski, R., Rodman, R., & Sheppard, K. (2004). Virtual limits: Multicultural dimensions of online dimensions. *International Educator, 12*(3), 30–39.

Godfrey, P. C., Illes, L. M., & Berry, G. R. (2005). Creating breadth in business education through service learning. *Academy of Service Learning and Education, 4,* 309–323.

Godkin, M. A., & Savagiau, J. A. (2001). The effect of a global multiculturalism track on cultural competence of preclinical medical students. *Family Medicine, 33,* 178–186.

Green, A. E. (2001). But you aren't white: Racial perceptions and service-learning, *Michigan Journal of Community Service Learning, 8*(1), 18–26.

Greenwald, S. R., & Rosner, D. J. (2003). Are we distance educating our students to death? Some reflections on the educational assumptions of distance learning. *Radical Pedagogy, 5*(1). Retrieved February 10, 2007, from: http://radicalpedagogy.icaap.org/content/ issue5_1/04_greenwald-rosner.html

Hacker, J.S. (2006). *The great risk shift: The assault on American jobs, families, health care, and retirement and how you can fight back.* New York: Oxford University Press.

Hackman, J. R., & Oldham, G. R. (1980). *Work redesign.* Upper Saddle River, NJ: Pearson Education.

Hatcher, J. A., Bringle, R. G., & Muthiah R. (2004). Designing effective reflection: What matters to service-learning? *Michigan Journal of Community Service Learning, 11*(1), 38–46.

Herring, S. C. (1992). *Gender and participation in computer-mediated linguistic discourse.* Washington, DC: ERIC Clearinghouse on Languages and Linguistics. (ERIC Document Reproduction Service No. ED345552)

Herring, S. C. (1993). Gender and democracy in computer-mediated communication. *Electronic Journal of Communication, 3*(2). Retrieved March 1, 2007, from: http://www.cios.org/ www/ejc/v3n293.htm (Reprinted in *Computerization and controversy* (2nd ed.), pp. 476–489, by R. Kling, Ed., 1996, New York: Academic Press.)

Herring, S. C. (2001). *Gender and power in online communication.* Retrieved March 1, 2007, from: http://rkcsi.indiana.edu/archive/CSI/WP/WP01-05B.html

Holland, B. (1997). Analyzing institutional commitment to service: A model of key organizational factors. *Michigan Journal of Community Service Learning, 4,* 30–41.

Howard, J. (1993). Principles of good practice for service-learning pedagogy. In J. Howard (Ed.), *Praxis I: A faculty casebook on community service learning* (pp. 3–12). Ann Arbor. MI: OCSL Press.

Howard, J.P.F., Gelmon, S.B., & Giles, D.E. Jr. (2000). From yesterday to tomorrow: Strategic directions for service-learning research [Special issue]. *Michigan Journal of Community Service Learning,* 5–10.

Huckin, T. (1997). Technical writing and community service. *Journal of Business and Technical Communication, 11*, 49–59.

Hudson, B. (2002). Critical dialogue online: Personas, covenants, and candlepower. In K. E. Rudestam & J. Schoenholtz-Read (Eds.), *Handbook of online learning* (pp. 53–90). Thousand Oaks, CA: Sage.

Jacoby, B. (1996). *Service-learning in higher education: concepts and practices.* San Francisco: Jossey-Bass.

James-Deramo, M. (1999). *Best Practices in cyber-serve: Integrating technology with service-learning instruction.* Blacksburg, VA: Virginia Tech Service Learning Center.

James-Deramo, M., & Macedo, P. (1999). Distance and service-learning in the sciences. M. James-Deramo (Ed.), *Best Practices in cyber-serve: Integrating technology with service-learning instruction* (pp. 39–47). Blacksburg, VA: Virginia Tech Service Learning Center.

Johnston, S. N. (1999). Practicing community through technology. In M. James-Deramo (Ed.), *Best practices in cyber-serve: Integrating technology with service-learning instruction* (pp. 49–62). Blacksburg, VA: Virginia Tech Service Learning Center.

Joinson, A. N., & Buchanan, T. (2001). Doing educational research on the internet. In C. R. Wolfe (Ed.), *Learning and teaching on the web* (pp. 221–242). San Diego, CA: Academic Press.

Kenworthy-U'Ren, A. L., & Peterson, T. O. (2005). Service-learning and management education: Introducing the "WE CARE" approach. *Academy of Management Learning and Education, 4*, 272–277.

Kenworthy-U'Ren, A., Petri, A., & Taylor, M.L. (2006). Components of successful service-learning programs: Notes from Barbara Holland, Director of the U.S. National Service-Learning Clearinghouse. *International Journal of Case Method Research & Application, 18*(2), 120–129.

Khan, B. (1997). Web-based instruction: What is it and why is it? In B. H. Khan (Ed.), *Web-based instruction* (pp. 5–18). Englewood Cliffs, NJ: Educational Technologies Publications.

Kiely, R. (2004). A chameleon with a complex: Searching for transformation in international service-learning. *Michigan Journal of Community Service Learning, 10*(2), 5–20.

Kleinman, G., Siegel, P., & Eckstein, C. (2002). Teams as a learning forum for accounting professionals. *Journal of Management Development, 21*, 427–460.

Ko, S., & Rosen, S. (2001). *Teaching online: A practical guide.* Boston: Houghton Mifflin.

Kolb, D. A. (1984). *Experiential learning: Experience as the source of learning and development.* Englewood Cliffs, NJ: Prentice-Hall.

Kozma, R. B. (1991) Learning with media. *Review of Educational Research, 61*(2), 179–211.

Kramarae, C., & Taylor, H. J. (1993). Women and men on electronic networks: A conversation or a monologue? In H. J. Taylor, C. Kramarae, & M. Ebben (Eds.), *Women, information technology + scholarship: Women, information technology, and scholarship colloquium* (pp 52–61). Urbana, IL: Center for Advanced Study.

Lan, W. Y., & Repman, J. (1995). The effects of social learning context and modeling on persistence and dynamism in academic activities. *Journal of Experimental Education, 64,* 53–67.

Livingston, J. (2003). *Metacognition: An overview.* (ERIC Document Reproduction Service No. ED474273)

Locke, E. A. (1968). Toward a theory of task motivation and incentives. *Organizational Behavior and Human Performance, 3,* 187–189.

Lou, Y., Abrami, P. C., & d'Apollonia, S. (2001). Small group and individual learning with technology: A meta-analysis. *Review of Educational Research, 71*(3), 449–521.

Lowery, D., May. D. L., Duchane, K. A., Coulter-Kern, R., Bryant, D., Morris, P. V., Pomery, J. G., & Bellner, M. (2006). A logic model of service-learning: Tensions and issues for further consideration. *Michigan Journal of Community Service Learning, 12*(2), 47–60.

Lunsford, A. (1991). The nature of composition studies. In E. Lindemann & G. Tate (Eds.), *An introduction to composition studies* (pp. 3–14). New York: Oxford University Press.

Malvey, D., & Hamby, E. (2005). *E-service learning: A pedagogic innovation in education.* Retrieved February 10, 2007, from: http://www.sloan-c.org/conference/proceedings/2005/ ppt/1127825899258.ppt

Martin, A., Seblonka, K., Tryon, E., Hilgendorf, A., Stoecker, R., & Nellis, M. (2007). *The challenge of short-term service learning.* Unpublished manuscript.

Maurrasse, D. J. (2001). *Beyond the campus: How colleges and universities form partnerships with their communities.* New York: Routledge.

McKay, V. C., & Rozee P. D. (2004). Characteristics of faculty who adopt community service learning pedagogy. *Michigan Journal of Community Service Learning, 10*(2), 21–33.

Mejias, U. (2006). Teaching social software with social software. *Innovate, 2*(5). Retrieved February 12, 2006, from: http://www.innovateonline.info/index.php?view=article&id=260

Merrill, M. D. (1998, April). Inside Technology. *Training, 25.*

Meyer, K. A. (2003). Face-to-face versus threaded discussions: The role of time and higher order thinking. *Journal of Asynchronous Learning Networks, 7*(1), 55–65.

Mills, S. D. (2001). Electronic journaling: Using the web-based, group journal for service-learning reflection. *Michigan Journal of Community Service Learning, 8*(1), 27–35.

Minton, T. M., & Willett, L. S. (2003). Student preferences for academic structure and content in a distance education setting. *Online Journal of Distance Learning Administration, 6*(1). Retrieved February 10, 2007, from" http://www.westga.edu/%7Edistance/ojdla/spring61/ minton61.htm

Mintz, S. D., & Hesser, G. W. (1996). Principles of good practice in service-learning. In B. Jacoby & Associates (Eds.), *Service-learning in higher education: Concepts and practices* (pp. 26–52). San Francisco: John Wiley & Sons.

Miron, D., & Moely, B. E. (2006). Community agency voice and benefit in service-learning. *Michigan Journal of Community Service Learning, 12*(2), 27–37.

Morrison, J. L. (2003). US higher education in transition [Electronic version]. *On the Horizon, 11*(1), 6–10.

National Service-Learning Clearinghouse. (2004). *Service-learning in: nursing: A bibliography.* Retrieved April 28, 2006, from: http://www.servicelearning.org/lib_svcs/bibs/he_bibs/ sl_nursing/index.php

Nichols, M. (2003). *A theory for eLearning.* Retrieved June 12, 2007, from: http://www.ifets.info/journals/6_2/1.pdf

Nisar, T.M. (2004). E-learning in public organizations. *Public Personnel Management, 33*(1), 79–88.

Oblinger, D. (2003). Boomers, gen-xers, & millennials: Understanding the new student. *Educause Review, 38,* 44–47.

Ogburn, F., & Wallace, B. (1998). Freshman composition, the internet, and service-learning, *Michigan Journal of Community Service Learning, 5*(1), 68–74.

O'Reilly, M., & Newton, D. (2002). Interaction online: Above and beyond requirements of assessment. *Australian Journal of Educational Technology, 18,* 57–70.

Ornatowski, C., & Bekins, L. K. (2004). What's civic about technical communication? Technical communication and the rhetoric of 'community.' *Technical Communication Quarterly, 13,* 251–256.

Palloff, R. M., & Pratt, K. (1999). *Building learning communities in cyberspace.* San Francisco: Jossey-Bass.

Palloff, R. M., & Pratt, K. (2003). *The virtual student: A profile and guide to working with online learners.* San Francisco: Jossey-Bass.

Park University vision. Retrieved June 24, 2007, from Park University Web site: http://www.park.edu/about/Description/mission.asp

Phipps, J. J. (2005). E-journaling: Achieving interactive education online. *Educause Quarterly, 28*(1), 62–65. Retrieved February 20, 2007, from: http://www.educause.edu/apps/eq/eqm05/eqm0519.asp?bhcp=1

Potter, P. A., & Perry, A. G. (2005). *Fundamentals of nursing* (6th ed.). St. Louis, MO: Mosby.

Porter, M., & Monard, K. (2001). *Ayni* in the global village: Building relationships of reciprocity through international service-learning. *Michigan Journal of Community Service Learning, 8*(1), 5–17.

Putnam, R. D. (2001). *Bowling alone: The collapse and revival of American community.* New York: Simon & Schuster.

Reich, R. (1992). *The work of nations: Preparing ourselves for the 21st century.* New York: Vintage Books.

Rifkin, J. (1996). *The end of work: The decline of the global labor force and the dawn of the post-market era.* New York: Putnam Books.

Rowe, N. C. (2004). Cheating in online student assessment: Beyond plagiarism. *Online Journal of Distance Learning Administration, 7*(2). Retrieved February 10, 2007, from: http://www.westga.edu/~distance/ojdla/summer72/rowe72.html

Rust, G., Kondwani, K., Martinez, R., Dansie, R., Wong, W., Fry-Johnson, Y., et al. (2006). A crash-course in cultural competence. *Ethnicity & Disease Journal, 16*(No. 2, Suppl. 3), S3-29–S3-36.

Sandy, M., & Holland, B. (2006). Different worlds and common ground: Community partner perspectives on campus-community partnerships. *Michigan Journal of Community Service Learning, 13*(1), 30–43.

Saulnier, B. (2005). Service-learning as an e-learning paradigm for technology higher education. *International Journal of Technology, Knowledge and Society, 2*(1), 80–89.

Schilling, P. (2005, December). Technology as epistemology. *Academic Commons.* Retrieved June 1, 2007, from: http://www.academiccommons.org/commons/essay/technology-as-epistemology

Schuler, D. (2004). Toward civic intelligence: Building a new sociotechnological infrastructure. In A. Feenberg & D. Barney (Eds.), *Community in the digital age: Philosophy and practice* (pp. 263–285). Lanham, MD: Rowman & Littlefield.

Schulman, S., Beisser, S., Larson, T. & Shelley, M. (2002). *Digital citizenship: Lessons learned as service-learning meets the digital divide.* Paper presented at the annual meting of the American Political Science Association. Retrieved June 2, 2007, from: http://www.allacademic.com/meta/p66312_index.html

Schwartz, N. H., Andersen, C., Hong, N., Howard, B., & McGee, S. (2004). The influence of metacognitive skills on learners' memory of information in a hypermedia environment. Journal of Educational Computing Research, 31(1), 77–93.

Senge, P. M., & Scharmer, O. (2001). Community action research: Learning as a community of practitioners, consultants and researchers. In P. Reason & H. Bradbury (Eds.), *Handbook of action research: Participative inquiry and practice* (pp. 238–249). London: Sage.

Shastri, A. (1999). *Investigating content knowledge gains in academic service-learning: A quasi-experimental study in an educational psychology course.* Paper presented at the annual meeting of the American Educational Research Association. Montreal, Quebec, Canada.

Silcox, H. (1995). *A how to guide to reflection: Adding cognitive learning to community service programs* (2nd ed.). Holland, PA: Brighton Press.

Slavin, R. E. (1983). When does cooperative learning increase student achievement? *Psychological Bulletin, 94,* 429–445.

Slavin, R. E. (1985). Team assisted individualization: A cooperative learning solution for adaptive instruction in mathematics. In M. Wang & H. Walberg (Eds.), *Adapting instruction to individual difference* (pp. 236–253). Berkeley, CA: McCutchan.

Slavin, R. E. (1986). *Using student team learning* (3rd ed.). Baltimore: Johns Hopkins University, Center for Research on Elementary and Middle Schools.

Sliwka, A., & Frank, S. (2004). Service Learning: Verantwortung lernen in Schule und Gemeinde [Service learning: Learning responsibility in school and community]. Weinheim und Basel, Germany: Beltz Verlag.

Sperling, R., Wang, V. O., Kelly, J. M., & Hritsuk, B. (2003). Does one size fit all? The challenge of social cognitive development. *Michigan Journal of Community Service Learning, 9*(2), 5–14.

Sroka, T. N. (2006). *Understanding the political influence of blogs: A study of the growing importance of the blogosphere in the U.S. Congress.* Retrieved Jun 20, 2007, from The George Washington University, Institute for Politics, Democracy, and the Internet Web site: http://www.ipdi.org/UploadedFiles/PoliticalInfluenceofBlogs.pdf

Stephenson, J. (Ed.). (2001). *Teaching and learning online: Pedagogies for new technologies.* London: Kogan Page.

Stevens, R. J., Madden, N. A., Slavin, R. E., & Farnish, A. M. (1986). *Cooperative integrated reading and composition: Two field experiments* (Tech. Rep. No. 7). Baltimore: Johns Hopkins University, Center for Research on Elementary and Middle Schools.

Stillman, L., & Stoecker, R. (2005). Structuration, ICTs, and community work. *Journal of Community Informatics, 1*(3), 83–102. Retrieved February 10, 2007, from: http://www.ci-journal.net/index.php/ciej/article/view/216

Stoecker, R. (2007). *Community organizations and service learning.* Retrieved February 10, 2007, from: http://comm-org.wisc.edu/sl

Strait, J. (1994). *Using portfolios as a method of developing metacognitive skills in college developmental readers.* Unpublished doctoral dissertation, University of Minnesota, Twin Cities.

Strait, J., & Sauer, T. (2004). Constructing experiential learning for online courses: The birth of e-learning. *Educause Quarterly, 1,* 62–65.

Strand, K., Marullo, S., Cutforth, N., Stoecker, R., & Donohue, P. (2003). *Community-based research in higher education: Methods, models and practice.* San Francisco: Jossey-Bass.

Tagliareni, M. E., & King, E. S. (2006). Documenting health promotion services in community-based nursing centers. *Holistic Nursing Practice, 20*(1), 20–26.

Tuckman, B. W. (1977). Stages of small group development revisited. *Group and Organizational Studies, 2,* 419–427.

Uchitelle, L. (2006). *The disposable American: Layoffs and their consequences.* New York: Alfred A. Knopf.

Vernon, A., & Ward, K. (1999). Campus and community partnerships: Assessing impacts & strengthening connections. *Michigan Journal of Community Service Learning, 6*(1), 30–37.

Vogelgesang, L.J. (2004). Diversity work and service-learning: Understanding campus dynamics, *Michigan Journal of Community Service Learning, 10*(2), 34–43.

Vonderwell, S. (2002). An examination of asynchronous communication experiences and perspectives of students in an online course: A case study. *The Internet and Higher Education, 6,* 77–90.

Vroom, V. H. (1964). *Work and motivation.* New York: John Wiley.

Warren, E., & Tvagi, A. W. (2003). *The two-Income trap: Why middle-class mothers and fathers are going broke.* New York: Basic Books.

Welsh, E. T., Wanberg, C. R., Brown, K. G., & Simmering, M. J. (2003). E-learning: Emerging uses, empirical results, and future directions. *International Journal of Training and Development, 7*(4), 245–258.

Westheimer, J., & Kahne, J. (2003, Winter). What kind of citizen? Political choices and educational goals. *Campus Compact Reader, 3,* pp. 1–13.

Wiley, J., & Schooler, J. W. (2001). The mental web—Pedagogical and cognitive implications of the net. In C. R. Wolfe (Ed.), *Learning and teaching on the web* (pp. 243–257). San Diego, CA: Academic Press.

Wink, D. M. (2001). Developing a community nursing center. *Nurse Educator, 26,* 70–74.

WordPress. (n.d.). Retrieved February 10, 2007, from: http://wordpress.org/

Printed in the United States
147957LV00002B/14/P

9 781593 119201